IN THEORY, DARLING

ALSO BY MARCOS GONSALEZ

Pedro's Theory: Reimagining the Promised Land

Revolting Indolence: The Politics of Slacking, Lounging, and Daydreaming in Queer and Trans Latinx Culture

IN THEORY, DARLING

SEARCHING FOR JOSÉ ESTEBAN MUÑOZ AND THE QUEER IMAGINATION

MARCOS GONSALEZ

Beacon Press, Boston

Beacon Press
Boston, Massachusetts
www.beacon.org

Beacon Press books
are published under the auspices of
the Unitarian Universalist Association of Congregations.

Printed in the United States of America

28 27 26 25 | 8 7 6 5 4 3 2 1

This book is printed on acid-free paper that meets the uncoated paper
ANSI/NISO specifications for permanence as revised in 1992.

*Library of Congress Cataloguing-in-Publication Data
is available for this title.*

Hardcover ISBN: 978-0-8070-0800-3
E-book ISBN: 978-0-8070-0801-1
Audiobook: 978-0-8070-1860-6

For Stephanie Hsu and Kandice Chuh,
who made learning theory pleasurable

CONTENTS

INTRODUCTION

STUDENT, PHD, PROFESSOR, THEORIST, STRANGER

It's all in my head. This imagined relation of intimacy. My fantasy of closeness to him. Never met, never known, never encountered flesh to flesh.

He is photographs on a computer screen, to me. He is a lecture recorded and uploaded onto the internet, to me. He is words on a page, to me.

I turn to the biographical record in an effort to feel near:

Born in Cuba in 1967 and raised in Hialeah, Florida. Cuban in the diaspora. Attended Sarah Lawrence College in New York, where he studied comparative literature. In his senior year he participated in what became known as the Westlands Sit-In of 1989, a student occupation of an administrative building in protest of racial inequities at the college. He went straight from undergrad to doctoral studies at Duke University, studying, once again, literature. There he studied with the renowned queer theorist Eve Sedgwick, who later became his friend. In 1994, he received his doctoral degree in literature and, at the age of twenty-six, became a professor of performance studies at New York University, where he would teach for nearly twenty years—an East Coaster through and through. In his lifetime he wrote articles, edited anthologies, and published two monographs. He gave his works memorable titles like "Feeling Brown, Feeling Down" and "Hope in the Face of Heartbreak." Never boring. His first book, *Disidentifications*, published in 1999, proposed his now well-known theory of disidentifying: how queers of color cleverly reclaim dominant stereotypes and abjection for political resistance and liberatory worldmaking. His second book, *Cruising Utopia*, published ten years after his first, made a big splash with its theorizations on queer utopianism and hope that expanded past the halls of academia, putting him on the radar of many scholars and non-scholars alike. His ideas contributed to various schools of thought like queer theory and critical race studies, with his work most generously helping to shape the formation of queer of color theory. He was made department chair in what would be his final years of life. He passed away in 2013. In 2020, his unfinished book-length project on brownness and Latino identity was published, *The Sense of Brown*.

More facts can be found. More facts presented. These facts are all I seem to have of him. But they do not create the closeness I desire. They do not alleviate the yearning I have to know more, be more.

In theory, he is nothing to me. I should not feel the pull to him. But I do not let that prevent me from feeling my imagined intimacy. It is mine, true and passionately felt. So, he is everything to me. This theorist of many, my stranger most intimate.

1

THE THEORY OF FALLING IN LOVE WITH THEORY

1. FIRST DATES

Return with me to the scene of the theorist as a college student: to José Esteban Muñoz in the late 1980s, before he's written his theories or published his treatises. Long before I've discovered the thrall of the theorist's words.

Home from college, the student watches a local Florida-area television program with his parents. He marvels at what he sees: a gay Cuban on the screen, Pedro Zamora. In a few years, Zamora will appear on MTV's *The Real World: San Francisco*, but the college student sees him before this fame. Zamora feels familiar to the college student, who was born in Havana and raised in the Cuban diasporic enclave of Hialeah, Florida. Zamora is one of the first people living with HIV/AIDS to be portrayed on US television. He gives not only a face to an illness that was purposefully made out to be a faceless boogeyman, but also a story, a rallying cry, a politics. When the college student sees Zamora on the screen, reaching out to him and his parents, the world shifts a little. Contemplation stirs.

Five years later, in his debut book, *Disidentifications: Queers of Color and the Performance of Politics*, the theorist will write of this first sighting of Zamora: "I was struck because this was something new. It was a new formation, a being for others."[1] The theorist will devote an entire chapter to Zamora, examining how he presented a defiant and out queer life on the television screen; how he reconfigured conceptions of queerness, Latinidad, and illness, challenging popular discourses that sought to constrain minoritized peoples, constructing what the theorist will call a "counterpublic." How Zamora's televised appearances allowed a queer of color world to emerge on primetime.

The college student is transformed by Zamora on the TV. Zamora, a future muse for the theorist's critical eye. The theorist not quite yet a theorist, awash in the television glow.

José Esteban Muñoz lounging on a couch watching television, prelude to the theorist he will become.

Queers and college go together like peanut butter and jelly. I'd call it serendipitous, the encounter a queer kid has when they first step foot on their college campus. They know, almost instinctively, change is upon them. All the new people they will meet, all the new situations they will be in. Out with the old, in with the new.

During my undergrad years in the 2010s, each time I returned to visit my family in my rural New Jersey hometown, I felt more and more different from them. Changed. I saw that the world wasn't as small as I'd once thought it was. What remained consistent, however, was watching television and films together as a family, plopped on our sunken-in couches. Our favorite genre: horror. We loved the spectacle of possession films. But now, even old favorites like the *Exorcist* were new experiences for me, altered by my liberal arts education. I searched for hidden meanings in the movies, found larger sociopolitical critiques. My family didn't mind these interpretive assays—they indulged me in my readings.

It was undeniable: College had morphed the small-town queer. My sensibility was brand-spanking new. I couldn't sit on the couch watching horror films and *not* practice what my very expensive (funded by an array of high-interest loans that I am still paying back, will always be paying back) English degree had been teaching me: to overanalyze everything and anything.

Queers love college because it's one of the first times in their lives when they are immersed in queerness. People experimenting with their sexualities and genders. Freaky hairstyles, piercings. Classes on literary postmodernism and the cultural significance of pop music. Hooking up in dorm-room boxes, making out in clandestine places on campus. Even the very strictly straight people dabble in the queer arts. College foments queerness. As it should.

I first read *Disidentifications* as a college student. The book is a series of short chapters on queer of color performance and art, with case studies on the likes of Jean-Michel Basquiat, Isaac Julien, Ela Troyano, and Félix González-Torres, among others. In *Disidentifications*, Muñoz introduces his titular theory, disidentification: a way for minoritized subjects, in his case queer of color ones, to reclaim stereotypes used by the dominant public sphere to vilify or discipline us. Disidentifying, as a critical process, allows the minoritized person to repurpose the stigmatized image, trope, or category in order to create new relations, new desires, new ways of configuring the world. Disidentifying is the queer femme child crafting an affirmative image of themselves from starlets watched on TV; the non-white artist reclaiming racist imagery in their work; a butch person taking hypermasculine garb and making it their own. Disidentifying hijacks dominant meanings and symbols, exposing them for what they are and repurposing them for alternative political imaginaries. By doing so, he writes, "disidentification is a step further than cracking open the code of the majority; it proceeds to use this code as a raw material for representing a disempowered politics or positionality that has been rendered unthinkable by the dominant culture."[2] Minoritarian subjects—a term he uses to designate marginalized peoples or areas of knowledge that stand in contrast to the majoritarian, or dominant group—work both within and outside the majoritarian sphere, making strategies of resistance and worldmaking practices.

I was introduced to the book not in its entirety but through an assigned excerpt in a queer theory course. I was an English major with a focus on literary criticism. I'd known early on that I wanted to make a career out of studying literature, find some way to pursue my passion for books—so I planned to become a teacher. My literary criticism focus required me to take several theory courses. I really didn't know what a theory course entailed. The word *theory* to me meant something amorphous, something that I wasn't quite sure how to define or describe. Theory: some hypothetical, unproven idea on a topic; there were conspiracy theories and also chaos theory, which the straight boys loved harping on about in the dorms. What role did theory play in the study of literature? Did we really need to apply some outside theoretical text to back up our readings?

My first theory course: Literary Theory 101. We moved through various schools of thought like new criticism, structuralism, deconstruction, psychoanalysis, postcolonial critique, and reader-response theory. We read the major theorists with whom literary scholars engaged: Roland Barthes, Jacques Derrida, Hortense Spillers, Louis Althusser, Gayatri Spivak, Edward Said, Karl Marx. We also read contemporary scholarly articles that married theory with close readings of literary texts. I had never read such writing before. The prose was ornate, tricky to parse in one pass, and I often did not know what they were saying exactly, even after several rereadings. The course was overwhelming, yet all of it—the syntactic difficulty, the critiques of dominant structures, the rereadings, the various methods for interpreting literature, the brain knots, the propositions for understanding the world differently, the Googling, the applying of concepts to a Toni Morrison novel or a Shakespeare play or whatever other canonical text in order to produce your own particular reading of it—left me hooked. I wanted more. When I saw a course offering in queer theory, I knew this was the next theory course I needed to take.

Queer theory had emerged in the 1990s as the unruly younger sibling of gay and lesbian studies. It seeks to theorize the complexities of sexuality, to challenge heteronormativity through the reclamation of negative affects like shame and even the term *queer*. The queer theory course that I took tracked many of the debates that had unfolded in the field since the 1990s, from Judith Butler's "gender as performance" to Lee Edelman's anti-relational turn away from reproductive futurity and embrace of queer negativity.

I greatly admired the professor who taught the class. She was the first woman of color professor I'd ever had, as well as the first out queer professor I'd known. Her course introduced us to a broad array of queer theorists and small excerpts from their works. Without a doubt, the famous white queer theorists were there on the syllabus: Jack Halberstam, Michel Foucault, Judith Butler, Eve Kosofsky Sedgwick. But the course also included, and prioritized, queer theorists of color like Roderick Ferguson, Mel Y. Chen, Jasbir Puar, and José Esteban Muñoz. Through those readings, and our professor's instruction, my classmates and I learned that analyses of sexuality and gender could not be divorced from race, nationality, ability, transness, or any other axes of social difference—that you cannot think of *queer* as separate from these other categories because notions of queerness have always been constituted and negotiated through other vectors, especially race.

Thinking in such a way was novel for me. I had always understood—or, rather, been made to understand—these categories as separate. I was a queer Mexican–Puerto Rican kid from a rural white farming town in New Jersey. I'd drunk and internalized the white-supremacy Kool-Aid for nearly twenty years by the time I entered the queer theory course. Self-hatred seethed from my pores, knowing that my undocumented Mexican father was a dark brown–skinned man, de-tribalized and Indigenous descended, a farmworker who could not read or write. From kindergarten through high school, my white classmates told me that men like him, and families like mine, were nothing. I went to New York City with this ideological inheritance, tried to make over who I was and where I came from. Failed, in the end, thankfully. New York, and queer theory, transformed me for the better.

José Esteban Muñoz was born in Cuba in 1967. My father was born a year before him, 1966, in Mexico. My father grew up in a family that, in exchange for the roof over their heads, worked the land of a rich estate owner. Muñoz was raised in Hialeah, Florida, his family having moved to the Cuban enclave when he was just a baby. Muñoz attended Sarah Lawrence for undergrad, Duke for doctoral study. My father never attended school. He needed to begin working in the fields at the age of six to help support his family. Muñoz was a professor of performance studies at New York University, and my father was a farmworker.

These two men, so important in my life, distant from each other yet connected by this nearness of birth, by these Latin American origins, by these differences that unify. Two theorists in their own regard, both dear to me.

A scholar who'd been a classmate of Muñoz's at Duke remembers the young theorist in this way: "In class he was mostly quiet, but when he did talk, he made his hands move strangely, elbows down, palms open, wrists twitching counterclockwise and then clockwise as if in refusal to be pinned down, while he hesitantly raised doubts about the text, about the conversation, about what we were actually doing there."[3] Like he was turning a doorknob on the ceiling, or screwing in a lightbulb, or signaling in code to an alien species.

I tend to believe the best ideas germinate when the gestures of the body behave peculiarly, perform their knowledge. Or maybe it's just what studious queers like to do in classrooms: maneuver our hands and arms in unusual gestures, act fabulous through embodied oddness. When I was a student speaking in a classroom, my limp-wristed hands were always flying across the air. I needed my hands to help make the point I was trying to make. I knocked down my iced coffee once, let the spill dribble down the table until I finished saying what I had to say. This embodied, communicative frenzy only got worse when I became a professor. My hands now whirlwind around my body, limbs and digits flailing, trying to imprint the lesson in question, making memorable big ideas, grand theories.

Words are never enough for the queer who loves, who thrives, in the classroom space. Learning is all about the body. Perform the ideas that need to be known.

2. FALLING HARD

In 2023, Florida Republican legislators rejected one of the College Board's latest Advanced Placement course offerings, AP African American Studies. Advanced Placement courses provide university-level curricula to high school students, and in many cases allow them to get college course credit. One of the reasons for the rejection of the AP African American Studies course: The curriculum included a unit on queer theory. It is inappropriate, the thin-skinned Republicans argue, to teach such material to high school students. It will turn kids gay, presumably, turn students into gender deviants challenging the norms of patriarchy. As if that were a bad thing. The Republicans also argued that queerness had no room in the study of African American life, culture, and history. Race, sexuality, and gender are separate and incommensurate categories, these Republicans believe. As do so many others.

......

I do not expect these Republicans to know or care what queer of color theory is. The field, established in the late 1990s and reaching maturity in the 2000s, was a counter to both the overwhelming whiteness that dominated mainstream queer theory and also the disregard of queer and trans analytics within ethnic studies. In short, the US academy was willfully overlooking race in studies of queerness and queerness in studies of race. Queer of color theory boldly declared that race, sexuality, gender, nationality, and class are always shaping and informing one another. Theorists like Juana María Rodríguez, Jasbir Puar, Mark Rifkin, K'eguro Macharia, C. Riley Snorton, Sarah Ahmed, and José Esteban Muñoz demonstrated how certain bodies (read: white, cisgender, heterosexual, able, monied) were configured as universal, as valuable, all the while erasing and making violable others. Syllabi were changed, new courses designed. "Queer of color analysis," writes Roderick A. Ferguson in his seminal, field-defining 2003 book of queer of color theorizing, *Aberrations in Black*, "shed[s] light on the ruptural components of culture, components that expose the restrictions of universality, the exploitation of capital, and the deceptions of national culture."[4] Jasbir Puar extends Ferguson's early work in books like *Terrorist Assemblages* and *The Right to Maim* by instructing us on how queer people have become incorporated into the US liberal nation-state—how they have proven useful in propagating homonormative ideologies that conjure the vision of a backwards, dangerous Arab Other that must be defeated for the sake of national "safety." Puar's work demonstrates how sexuality and race are set against one another, purposefully manipulated by state power to help produce expendable non-white populations. Queer of color theory is not just about affirming queer of color life and thought; it also provides tools for exposing and resisting the machinations of power through analyses that factor in the ever-evolving complexities of race, gender, and sexuality.

Many of these queer of color theorists were in dialogue with one another as their ideas and scholarship developed. Their network spanned countries and continents. They mentored a generation of students that would continue their important work. Each theorist has expanded the scope of what is thinkable when we conceive of sexuality, gender, and race in the world we live in. The Kenyan theorist K'eguro Macharia reminds us that it is important not to think of queer theory and studies as solely belonging to the Global North. As Macharia articulates it: "The work of thinking through queer Africa will be mostly illegible to US and European ears trained by and embedded in LGBTI studies. Or, as is happening too often, queer African voices and experiences will be absorbed as 'data' or 'evidence,' not as modes of theory or as challenges to the conceptual assumptions that drive queer studies."[5] Here, Macharia affirms the importance of queer African thinkers generating their own concepts and theories without having to fit into preexisting frameworks or be mined for the interests of Global North scholars. Queer theory looks different from place to place and deserves to flourish everywhere. Or, as Muñoz formulated in a cowritten introduction to a special issue of *Social Text* in 1997, "*queer* as a point of departure for a broad critique that is calibrated to account for the social antagonisms of nationality, race, gender, and class *as well as* sexuality."[6]

Queer of color theory, in practice, incentivizes modes of theorizing, world building, and creating through queer of color experiences, histories, and aesthetics. It asserts that queer of color people and cultures can be the sites through which we analyze society. It reminds us that race, sexuality, and gender inform one another in complex ways that demand careful attention, and that are not just the provenance of academics and universities. Queer of color theory does not manifest only in jargon-filled language or peer-reviewed papers. It is also about everyday living.

Through Muñoz's writing in particular, I saw how movies, bars, clubs, performances, poems, gestures, plays, visual art forms, and absurdist installation pieces were all, in their own specific ways, theory. They generated thought, sparked ideas, helped us rethink reality. The highbrow mixed with the low, the abstract with the concrete, the joyous with the sad. They were theory because they demanded a systematized and contemplative approach to thinking through how they functioned. They required interpretation, analysis, and explanation for what they did in the world. From then on out, I was able to see how, for instance, a novel like Justin Torres's *We the Animals*, and the subsequent film adaption of it, were theorizations on queer of color and Puerto Rican pain and joy. Or how the 2016 film *Moonlight* was pure theory, a filmic exploration of the dimensions of Black queer childhood. Even photographs and home videos of my queer childhood self became sites of theoretical inquiry. All around me, the world was opening up. I recognized in new ways things that had already been speaking to me as theory but that I hadn't identified as such because I had been taught since childhood that theorizing was what white, monied people did. Thinking critically, and getting paid and supported to think critically, was not something that people like me did or were supposed to do. Those few in the ivory towers in the United States and Europe dictated who was a theorist, what was legitimate theory, what were worthy sites of theorization. The rest of us had no right to produce theory, or to be theory. I believed this until I read Muñoz.

In grad school, during the mid-2010s, I once participated in a heated debate. The professor didn't know what to do. That day, each student was giving a brief presentation on a theorist who had shaped their own work. My choice: Muñoz. I talked about how his thinking had allowed me to see how queer people of color can create knowledge, and how our knowledge can help create a better world. I also mentioned how it was nice to have a queer Latinx scholar who had made such an impact on queer theory. It was sentimental, a mood most academics shy away from.

After I concluded, another student, a white queer, had, as he put it, a "few comments." He said that he did not understand—as someone who had rigorously studied queer theory and engaged with the likes of Foucault, Bersani, and Edelman (all of whom happen to be white)—what queer theory had to say about the study of race.

My blood pressure rose. His response was typical of many white academics of the time. They feared that these new considerations of race were impinging on established studies of gender, sexuality, and class—fields they had shored up a lot of power and prestige in.

I gave him a lecture. He grew noticeably upset at how heated I was. He kept insisting that queer theory, and queer studies in general, should not have to consider race or be about race.

"Every text and author you study is white," I replied. "Do you think their whiteness has no bearing on how they live in the world or how the world treats them?"

He couldn't answer properly. Wasn't his fault, really; he lived in a society that had never taught him how to account for, to even think about, whiteness and white supremacy. All eyes were on us. He fumbled his words, became so flustered that his only comeback, the only means of one-upping me, had to be to just say the quiet part out loud: "I don't know why everything has to be about race."

Muñoz made it about race in a brief 2005 essay critiquing the original *Queer Eye for the Straight Guy*. Here, as in *Disidentifications*, he turns to reality television to understand the racialized realities of queer life. He observes how the show equates queerness with whiteness through the tokenization of the only Fab Five member of color, Jai Rodriguez. Rodriguez is the culture expert of the group (much like Karamo Brown in the 2018 series reboot), whose role is to add zest and color to the group's glaring, yet unmarked, whiteness. "In neoliberalism's gay formations, race is 'merely cultural' and therefore a kind of symbolic surplus value,"[7] Muñoz concludes. Non-white queerness is festive window dressing under rainbow capitalism, a way to zhuzh up a queerness that knows itself as white, glorifies itself as white, but plays demure in saying so.

Even before *Disidentifications*, Muñoz had already zeroed in on the dominance that whiteness holds over queer sociality and cultural production. In a 1998 article titled "Dead White," Muñoz reviewed three films—*Jeffrey*, *Frisk*, and *Safe*—from the New Queer Cinema movement of the early '90s. This movement was defined by an increase in independent queer films that put queer life and sexuality front and center. He riffs on the way that journals dedicate special issues to topics like "race" and "queerness," showing how some of these films "make whiteness a special issue. Whiteness in these films is a slippery thing, not reducing to a single set of mechanisms but calling attention to its universalizing and camouflaging properties."[8] Muñoz praises these films for how they expose whiteness rather than presenting it as unmarked and universal.

In a 1998 essay, cowritten with John Vincent, Muñoz analyzes two films by Gus Van Sant, *Mala Noche* (1985) and *My Own Private Idaho* (1991). Both films feature straight hustlers, or "trade," and the primary focus of the essay is on how the fetishized Mexican immigrant male body stands in for US–Latin America relations. Here they articulate how "the Latino body also signifies a crisis within the normative white U.S. gay male culture."[9] It is "an object that does not lack agency but instead is characterized by its use of agency to camouflage itself or let itself be transformed under the revisionary aegis of the Other's gaze."[10] The Latino body adapts in order to get by and, sometimes, to get what they want, even under white supremacy. Muñoz's work has from the beginning advocated for critiquing whiteness and white supremacy as a project of queer studies. More importantly, he did not see queers of color as passive victims of structural inequities but rather as creators, resistors, and innovators capable of enacting social change and political transformation. From his earliest writings he imagined queer people of color as the doers and producers of theory itself when few others did.

Queer of color life and aesthetics have always been seen as consumable by the mainstream white queer establishment and the general culture. We need look no further than the now widely popular film *Paris Is Burning* (1990), which documents the ball and house culture built by African American, Afro-Latinx, and non-Black Latinx trans and queer folks in 1980s New York. The ballroom scene had first emerged there in the 1970s, where various houses formed to compete against one another in categories like "fem realness" and "butch realness." Ballroom culture generated dance styles like vogueing, and now-popular sayings like "throwing shade." Through the decades, white queer people and cishet people of color became interested in ball culture for its extractive potential—for the quips, gestures, sass, and dancing that could help them stand out. Madonna became a case in point—her popular 1990 song "Vogue" was inspired by ballroom voguing and house music. Not many fans seemed to care to learn anything more about queer of color communities beyond the fun commentary and great dancing they provided. The film *Paris Is Burning*, mentioned frequently on shows like *RuPaul's Drag Race* and screened in college classrooms across the world, has become so pervasive and embedded into our culture that people no longer realize that these forms and styles of ballroom culture originated with trans and queer people of color. Shows like *Pose* and *Legendary* have helped to rectify the oversight caused by the commodification of the documentary. Over time, however, with constant repetition, ballroom culture has been appropriated into the general "queer culture," losing the historical specificity and material labor that created it. And if you are a non-white queer person, you are under pressure to be a cultural innovator, theatrical, and over-the-top.

The graduate student who told me "I don't know why everything has to be about race" avoided me at all costs after our debate. I had already ruined his race-free bubble enough.

"Much of queer theory nowadays sounds like a metanarrative about the domestic affairs of white homosexuals," quipped Muñoz and co-editors, Jack Halberstam and David L. Eng, in the introduction to a 2005 special issue of *Social Text*.[11]

In addition to reality TV, talk shows also made their way into Muñoz's first book. He provides an anecdote of himself as a child, staying up past his bedtime to watch late night television: "I remember, for instance, seeing an amazingly queeny Truman Capote describe the work of fellow writer Jack Kerouac as not writing but, instead, typing. I am certain that my pre-out consciousness was completely terrified by the swishy spectacle of Capote's performance. But I also remember feeling a deep pleasure in hearing Capote make language, in 'getting' the fantastic bitchiness of his quip."[12]

The queer kid in rapt attention at the televised queerness. After-bedtime talk-show watching as part of his identity formation. Televised bitchiness a theoretical site of possibility.

Sometimes unsaid, sometimes implied, and most often thought, the reigning question on the minds of Republicans, and many white people in the United States for that matter: "I don't know why everything has to be about race."

Though Muñoz is spot on about the problems inherent in *Queer Eye for the Straight Guy*, I nonetheless enjoyed the series growing up. I watched the show only when my family wasn't around, or when they were asleep. It was where I first saw out and proud queer people on television. Well, anywhere really. I did not identify with them in the conventional sense of the term. Their well-established careers, their style, their posh city lives, were all far removed from my country bumpkin reality. Rather, I saw them as models for what queer embodiment and attitude could look like. I wanted to move through the world as they did: confident and unbothered, free to be flaming, to be too much, to not give a damn what others think.

Like Muñoz, I also grew up watching *The Real World*. I watched such reality shows for entertainment, of course, but also to find snatches of possibility for a queer life that I felt I had yet to live. On the small screen I looked for queer people flirting and hooking up in messy abandon so that I could know what it felt like to be desired, lusted after, touched. I looked for queer people who had queer friends, to get a sense of what queer friendship was like, the mechanics that made such intimacies flourish, or founder. I looked for queer people who were living and breathing because the child I was needed those testaments that queer adulthood was something I could aspire to, that was livable. I searched on television for a sense of self I had yet to know, but I at least knew I needed. Maybe this is what compelled Muñoz to reality television. Maybe he needed to see Pedro Zamora then and there in order to know a queer life was livable, too.

I'm struck by the autobiographical flourishes in *Disidentifications*. The bringing in of the queer child and the college student, the television as a site of thought. These moments felt extraordinary. There I was, reading something called Theory, something that I did not associate with the autobiographical, did not associate with people with subjectivities like mine. In my early undergraduate years, I had a preconception that theory was supposed to be objective, from an identity-less universal standpoint, and about highly abstract concepts. Most especially, theory was done by white people of means in their ivory towers. I enjoyed reading theorists like Derrida, Barthes, and Foucault, all of those French men, but couldn't ignore the fact they derived from similar backgrounds and coteries. But there he was, the queer Cuban Muñoz, the theorist as college student. *Disidentifications*, when I first encountered it, felt like an unthinkable book. I could not think that something like it was possible, did not think such thinking was possible. Until it was.

I relish how much critical attention Muñoz gave to television. He gave us couch potatoes hope that we, too, could wax philosophical.

Television made me queer before any theory.

3. LOVE COMEDOWN

Eve Kosofsky Sedgwick, the acclaimed queer theorist who taught Muñoz while he was a doctoral student at Duke, who also became his friend, once wrote, "The most compelling thing about obituaries is how openly they rupture the conventional relations of person and address."[13]

......

I never met Muñoz. Though there were three years when we were both living in New York City, our paths never crossed. He died in 2013, during my junior year of undergrad. His death was sudden and unexpected, taking him from us too soon. He had been working in the performance studies program at New York University, one of the doctoral programs I wanted to apply to because he was in it. I wanted to study with the theorist whose work meant so much to me, whose ideas had transformed me. But by the time I was submitting applications, he had already passed. I was no longer interested in NYU because he was no longer there. I went to another program, a different path, another story.

Muñoz cites Sedgwick throughout his work. In books, in articles, in passing. The mentor everywhere. "Eve Kosofsky Sedgwick has not only been an extraordinary dissertation director," he notes in his acknowledgments to *Disidentifications*, "but also an invaluable friend. I continue to be inspired by her work, her example, and her presence."[14] The references are adoringly professional, doting upon her brilliance. He interweaves his serious intellectual engagements with the theories of his teacher, in dialogue with her. The frequency with which he cites and acknowledges Sedgwick speaks to the importance of the teacher on the student, to how transformative that bond can be. Citations: a gesture of love.

His *New York Times* death notice reads: "Extraordinary teacher and writer of astonishing grace, José was particularly adept at seeing beauty where others sometimes failed to discern it: in the face of his beloved French bulldog Lydia, in the vulnerable flounderings of the queer downtown performance artists he loved, and in his enormous circle of friends on, as he put it, 'the island of misfit toys.'"[15]

The professor who taught my undergraduate queer theory course also happened to be a former student of Muñoz. She told me this after

I'd shared with her my desire to apply to doctoral programs. Performance studies was at the top of my list, because of Muñoz, and she aided me in assembling my application. Soon thereafter, she approached me on campus. Her face was grim, eyes exuding a doe-like sadness. José Muñoz died, she said. Before I could even submit the application to his department, he was gone.

Muñoz was forty-six when he passed away. In his lifetime he only published two books, some articles, and a few reviews. His third book, which he was working on at the time of his death, would be published posthumously in 2020. Eve Sedgwick, in comparison, published many books, essays, and poems during her lifetime. Her time on earth was longer—fifty-eight years. Her oeuvre seems immense in contrast to his. We have so much of her, and so little of him.

If he'd had more time, he probably would have experimented with the form of his writing, as his teacher had with hers. He surely would have developed upon his prior ideas, giving new life to the old. He certainly would have theorized in new directions and with different texts and objects, if he'd had the chance. When I think of Muñoz, I think about what he would have created. I think about the loss of his future ideas.

A detail about Muñoz I'd never known: the French bulldog, Lydia.

In her face he saw beauty where so many saw the contrary.

In 2009, Eve Sedgwick died from cancer, four years shy of Muñoz's 2013 passing. Teacher and student, later friends, so close to one another in death. I'm not sure why exactly this proximity startles, but it does.

After learning from my professor of Muñoz's death, I didn't grieve him. I felt sad, yes, and disappointed that I would never get the chance to work with him in any capacity. I couldn't feel the grief my professor was experiencing. I don't necessarily feel grief now, years later writing this. There's something about the word *grief* that I ascribe to the familiar: those we knew personally, who entered and exited our lives, those who we can never stop thinking about. The French theorist Roland Barthes exemplifies this in his books *Camera Lucida* and *Mourning Diary*, which focus upon his dead mother, Henriette. The theorist theorizes his mother's death because he can't get over that she is gone. He theorizes his grief in order to allay it, sometimes putting it plainly: "Don't say *Mourning*. It's too psychoanalytic. I'm not *mourning*. I'm suffering."[16] No matter how much philosophizing he does, Barthes can't seem to live without his mother. Ink and paper cannot quell his grief, the suffering too immense for another to fathom.

If it's not grief exactly that I feel over Muñoz, then what is it? His words and ideas changed my life. I have felt his impact upon me. I have lost a familiar stranger. Someone who recognized me for all that I am before any other person in my life. A queer Latinx predecessor who paved the way for people like me to live the life of the mind.

The loss too much to describe.

In the acknowledgments of Muñoz's second monograph, *Cruising Utopia: The Then and There of Queer Futurity*, we read: "Eve Kosofsky Sedgwick passed as I finished this book. She has been my great friend and mentor. Her gentle touch and luminous inspiration is everywhere for me."[17]

Barthes' mother died in 1977, aged eighty-four. He followed her to the grave shortly thereafter in 1980, aged sixty-five.

"There I was, alone in the apartment where she had died," he writes, "looking at these pictures of my mother, one by one, under the lamp, gradually moving back in time with her looking for the truth of the face I had loved. And I found it."[18]

There is a picture of Muñoz in a turtleneck that now lives on the internet. It's a black-and-white portrait. He is young, an outlier among all the other Muñoz photos that circulate, most from his later life in the 2000s and early 2010s. This one has to be from the late 1980s or early '90s—he can't be any older than thirty. He looks up at the camera, softly smirking, a head of curls. His eyes inquisitive, boyish. Charming, a catch. He looks like a member of a pop-rock band.

My fondness for the photo resides in its ability to mystify me. I know little about any of the Muñozes that I see in his photos, and even less about this young, turtlenecked Muñoz. I glance at the photo and believe he is the college student who makes a cameo in *Disidentifications*. Who returns to visit his parents, who watches reality television, who theorizes on the couch. He keeps me at arm's length with his smirk. He plays hard to get.

Barthes finds the truth about his mother in a photo from her childhood. The old photo is now famously referred to as the Winter Garden picture and, in his treatise on photography, *Camera Lucida*, he will call the truth of this photo *the punctum*: the detail that punctures the viewer, drawing their attention above all else, striking profoundly with meaning. Barthes writes of how he sees in the little girl, who is not yet his mother, the features that will later distinguish themselves as uniquely her: the expressions of her face, the placement of her hands, the pose of her body. All are early evidence of the kindness and gentleness he will associate with his mother. This punctum effect, he writes, "achieved for me, utopically, *the impossible science of the unique being*"[19] like a punch across space and time. The punctum is the striking detail of singularity. Your singular truth ascribed to the photo.

Though Barthes's punctum reveals a truth about his mother, it also estranges him from her. The Winter Garden picture is both his mother and not his mother. She has not yet given birth to him; she has not yet become the woman he will know. He is no one to her. In the world of the photo, he does not exist. So Barthes must meet that little girl that is his mother elsewhere, in her dying: "During her illness, I nursed her, held the bowl of tea she liked because it was easier to drink from than from a cup; she had become my little girl, uniting for me with that essential child she was in her first photograph."[20] He had become his mother's mother.

There is an aura of intimacy to the photo of Muñoz in a turtleneck. As if a friend had taken it, a friend who may also have been a photographer. A softness permeates the black-and-white image. Maybe this is what induces the soft smirk and eyes. He is looking back at someone he knows. Loves? The snapshot from a familiar lens, a photographic caress.

Study reanimates the dead. It carries them into our present, for ourselves and others. The past is no coffin when we commit to studies of the dead. We bring them back to us, near us, when we learn how to care for them through concerted attention. Analysis is a love language.

Is the turtleneck photo taken before or after he moves to New York City in 1994 to become a professor of performance studies? Or is he still a doctoral student at Duke, studying with Sedgwick? Marc Anthony in the early '90s wore turtlenecks just like the one Muñoz wears. The theorist looks like a salsa singer from one of the many album covers from my mother's collection. The date of the photo eludes me.

"I'm fond of observing how obsession is the most durable form of intellectual capital," Sedgwick remarks in the introduction to her book, *Touching Feeling*.[21] Our obsessions—those things we can't stop thinking about, inquiring over, being hailed by—lead the intellectual down their path. Obsession drives the intellect. This essay collection was the last book she would publish in her lifetime, in 2003. Ten years prior, in a 1993 preface to her *Between Men*, Sedgwick had made a similar declaration: "Obsessions are the most durable form of intellectual capital."[22] Her 2003 version in *Touching Feeling* was a slight remixing, a renewing for another audience. Obsessed over obsessing over one's obsessions.

Turtlenecked Muñoz, young visage staring up and over, smacked lips smirking, the curled splendor atop his head—the photo enlivens the past, for my here and now.

4. A LOVE LIKE THIS

I read theory at the gay bar. How do you do it, a friend asks. The cackles all around me, limning maniacal, the lust stares, the loud playing of Britney and Madonna, the overall commotion of queer people congregating—all have certainly led to distraction many times. For me, though, the busy ambience is what precisely makes the environment hospitable to my pastime. Theory can be difficult, abstruse, can bend you into a thought-pretzel, and the gay bar offsets that. It sets me—excuse the expression—straight.

The hunky white daddy bartender asks me about the book I'm reading (well, technically, rereading), his curiosity piqued by the cover with its image of the Black Mexican American performance artist Vaginal Davis. She wears a long electric-blonde wig, no clothes to her name, and sits with her knees tightly put together. Her head is cocked slightly to the side and her rouged lips are parted, exposing her front teeth. She looks off to the side, with a face expressing bewilderment.

The book's title: *Disidentifications*.

This was my first true love.

In her 1991 essay "Theory as Liberatory Practice," bell hooks examines how theory helped her understand the pain she had experienced in her life. Theory was a source of healing: "I came to theory desperate, wanting to comprehend—to grasp what was happening around and within me."[23] Theory allowed her to understand the world. Theory helped her find a way to transform it.

Theory would serve the same function for me—help me grapple with suffering that felt insurmountable. In the early years of my adolescence, I fawned over white boys. Not exclusively, but my predominately white hometown made them readily available. My first crush was a white boy. He was a pale-as-milk, scrawny kid with a screechy laugh. I was nearly four times his height and weight, a gargantuan barrio kid. I lusted for him throughout middle and high school. I imagined our unevenly proportioned bodies making love, passionately, in scenes worlds away from the detached, anonymous sex I would come to know when I moved to New York. I imagined us married before gay marriage was even legal. I thought of the cute kids we would have (adopt). I pictured the holidays with his very cookie-cutter middle-class military white family (probably Republicans), and how normal they all would be in comparison to my poor-as-dirt and discombobulated Mexican–Puerto Rican family.

This boy represented all that I wasn't and couldn't be.

I loved the idea of him so spectacularly.

This fawning took some time to unpack.

It took an encounter with Muñoz, with theory.

Theory allowed me to understand why that white boy I'd doted on in high school—a boy I thought was my friend and who I thought could be more than my friend—wouldn't invite me to his house. I'd wanted to be invited in, could not understand the difference between us that necessitated my never-invite. Theory revealed all the ugliness behind why I'd aspired to be like him and his family, why I'd needed the validation of white boys and their white families. Theory exposed my self-hatred and pinpointed the roots of it. I'd suffered for so long, loving all that this white boy symbolized and hating all that I and my family symbolized, not knowing a way out.

Theory gave me a renewed sense of life: the processes of critical reflection and contemplation, the affirmation of inquiry as valuable, the excavation of self and world, the fact that everything and anything could be put under the microscope of scrutiny and analysis.

Theory told me I was not alone in this suffering, and that I did not have to be. Theory showed me how the world could be something else entirely from what it had to be. Theory was liberation.

I've never been one to fall in love easily. I had crushes in high school; in college I had various romantic prospects that never panned out. The first time I experienced a sensation one could call love was around the age of twenty-two. We met on an app. He was meant to be a hookup, a night or two of passionate sex, but he turned into something more. Boyfriend, eventually. This relation between the boy and me became unwieldy, all-encompassing. I couldn't get him off my mind. I couldn't unthink him and I knew, then, that it was love.

But there had been someone before this boy of flesh. I didn't know it then but I now know full well that I had loved a man I'd come to know in the pages of his book. A man made of paper and words, concepts and theories I could pick apart, an immaterial man I could think about constantly, without the all-too-real threat that real-life boyfriends bring. My boyfriend the theorist stayed fixed on the page. Comforted me when I wanted him to. Let me build on his words when I so desired. My private affair.

"Teaching, Minoritarian Knowledge, and Love," is a brief meditation by Muñoz on his love of teaching theory, published in 2004. "I want to think about my teaching as a 'putting into action' of theory," he posits.[24] In his view, the teaching of theory must also always be about the failures that abound in teaching: "Minoritarian production is an impossible project. Within majoritarian institutions the production of minoritarian knowledge is a project set up to fail. Mechanisms ensure that the production of such knowledge 'misfires' insofar as it is misheard, misunderstood, and devalued. Politics are only possible when we acknowledge that dynamic."[25] One must be honest about the nature of the work at hand in order to be the most effective teacher. To know the countless odds stacked against you when you teach underfunded, undersupported knowledges like queer of color critique or ethnic studies or trans theory—those areas of knowledge that diagnose the insufficiencies of the present and strive for alternatives, that yearn for another sense of the world. The love of teaching tempered by the reality that is twenty-first-century capitalism. If you don't acknowledge those realities you will burn out. You won't make a single modicum of difference if your idealism isn't adjusted to survive and persist within the existing power structures. You won't be able to aspire, as Muñoz did, after "helping others come into their own as not only speaking subjects, also professing subjects," which is, he wrote, "the ultimate stake of my pedagogy."[26]

My first copy of *Disidentifications*—a relic from my college years—is virtually unreadable. From beginning to end, in blue, yellow, and pink, I highlighted. Insatiable, I had to have been, pressing the highlighter's tip so hard the neon colors bled through the pages. My younger self equated highlighting with understanding. At the time I was unable to fully process what each sentence was saying, so I believed highlighting would help me learn. There were historical contexts and academic debates I did not yet know, sentences and words I could not yet parse. No amount of highlighting would help me in any of these regards, but I was adamant. "Desire is part of the scene of reading theory," Jordan Alexander Stein notes, "and desire is unruly."[27] I desired intensely a knowledge from that book.

I no longer highlight my books, having graduated to underlining and notes in the margins. But I look back to this copy with fondness for how much my younger self needed those words. So much so that I hoped highlighting would imprint them into me. Neon everlasting.

Although I consume both reality television and theory, I'm under no illusions about which is more popular: The first is seen as pleasurable, mindless, and easy to understand, whereas the second is boringly displeasing, demanding, and difficult. Of course more people watch reality television than read theory. Theory can't compare to the entertainment value of *Big Brother*, to any of the myriad versions of *Real Housewives*, to the drunken antics of *Jersey Shore*.

But the gap between reality television and theory is a difference of degree, not kind. Reading theory requires study, but so do the prospects of the various *Big Brother* contestants, the subtexts of dating, the reasons men do what they do, or any other seemingly inane topic. Attention must be paid. We know how to derive pleasure and joy from watching reality television because it's served up on a silver platter. Reality television gives it to us fast, in big bites that are effortlessly digestible. Reality television has drama and rivalry, riveting scenes and explosive exchanges that catch the attention, plot structure. You can't look away—you only want to watch more. Theory, on the other hand, dishes itself out incrementally, in morsels that require rigorous chewing, and often our palettes don't immediately know how to respond to the pleasures being served up. Our attentions wane. We yearn for a plot to rivet us. We can recognize a moment of revelation when a theorist articulates an idea in a particularly catchy way. We can reread a passage that we partly understood the first time around, the repetition helping to connect several loose strings of thought. But when words and ideas perplex us on the surface, make us feel "dumb," like we need to read ten other things first in order to understand the context, we shut down. A natural response in such a scenario. The confrontation not only discomforts—it insults. Humans yearn to know the why of things, and if we can't immediately get to the bottom of it, we quit, avoiding hurt feelings and bad sentiments. Seeing intellectual challenge as an affront is a tendency as old as time.

The problem with a capitalist society is that it leaves us so little time outside the labor-driven death drive upholding it. Most of our lives are, regrettably, spent working or worrying over money. We have little enough time as it is to devote to the things we enjoy, like reality television or theory. Studying theory requires a level of attention that only time, and a rested mind and body, can provide. Capitalism makes sure our bodies are so tired from laboring that we have no time to learn or appreciate anything, most especially something like theory. Why would it? So much of what we call *theory* actively traffics in critiques of capitalism.

It is easier to indulge in the messy simplicities of reality television, to scroll through an endless feed of social media posts, to be mesmerized by people livestreaming on TikTok doing bizarre, mind-numbing things because these activities turn time liquid. Time comes and goes smoothly. It is not our enemy in these scenarios. But when we read theory—and when we must reread, or when we stumble in thought, or do anything that challenges or discomforts or resists us—we are reminded of the preciousness of our time and energy. We have so little of either to give. The manufactured scarcity of both under capitalism induces that tiring, banal confrontation we all have with ourselves, far too frequently. Capitalism controls all relations, makes or breaks us. For most of the world's population, it breaks.

Like reality television, theory has its pleasures. Both are chock-full of aha-moments, of confoundingly inexplicable scenarios.

After Muñoz, after the impossible.

I am sleuthing across his oeuvre—the historical facts, the minor details of a life lived—for what, exactly? I cannot name precisely what I search for. Sedgwick allays some of my anxiety, reassures me that my search does not demand a precise goal: "There's a built-in gracelessness to the expectation that *any* essay will end with an explanation of exactly what it is that the writer is 'calling for,'" a posturing, "as if critical practices were ready-made consumer items among which one had only to choose."[28] I pilfer this sentence from her introduction to the anthology *Novel Gazing*, a volume of essays on queer readings of novels, which she edited. The introduction is titled "Paranoid Reading and Reparative Reading; or, You're So Paranoid, You Probably Think This Introduction Is About You." A few years later she adapted it into a standalone essay, "Paranoid Reading and Reparative Reading; or, You're So Paranoid, You Probably Think This

Essay Is About You." The essay has become far more widely known than the introduction that preceded it, and it also omits the sentence I quoted above, excises the idea I needed to hear: this need to think out loud with a net cast ambitiously wide, aimlessly catching my bits and my strands, compiling my own private dossier on Muñoz without pre-fixed goal in mind. It is a mode of being with Muñoz that finds traction in Wayne Koestenbaum's apt description of Sedgwick's style: "Her nonspecificity sometimes tied me up, prompted me to impugn my own hunger for literality. Perhaps it was the half-discernible presence of the specific within the foggy nonspecific that constituted the formidable, mind-teasing allure of her critical movements."

I construct this collage of words, my encounters with him through excerpts read in a class, through a book profusely highlighted, a mosaic of abstraction—of us?

"A motive I think everyone who does gay and lesbian studies is haunted by the suicides of adolescents," wrote Sedgwick in her 1993 essay collection, *Tendencies*.[29] Muñoz reworked his mentor's sentence in an essay published in his 1996 coedited anthology on Andy Warhol's queerness, *Pop Out*—this essay later incorporated into *Disidentifications*. His reframing accounts for queerness and non-whiteness at a time when the queer theoretical landscape conceptually left no room for the two to make contact: "I always marvel at the ways in which nonwhite children survive a white supremacist U.S. culture that preys on them. I am equally in awe of the ways in which queer children navigate a homophobic public sphere that would rather they did not exist. The survival of children who are both queerly and racially identified is nothing short of staggering."[30]

Muñoz's reformulation isn't a critique of Sedgwick. It is an extension of her thought, a loving riff born of the need to account for the queer child of color in queer theory. Juana María Rodríguez, discussing the famed queer theorist Lee Edelman's theorization of the racially unmarked child in a queer theory staple, *No Future*, poignantly points out "how children of color function as the co-constitutive symbolic nightmare of our nation's future," and "are never the imagined future subjects of the nation, and the forms of disciplinary power these children inspire operate differentially not only at the level of the symbolic, but also at the level of the material and juridical."[31] Both mentor and student are mobilized by the need to value queer children in queer politics. Both theorists affirm how queer theory can help envision a world where queer children not only exist, not only survive, but flourish.

This two-sentence version of Sedgwick's formulation is found in another essay included in an anthology published the same year as *Tendencies*: "A motive. I think everyone who does gay and lesbian studies is haunted by the suicides of adolescents."[32] A variation on a theme. In this version, a period has been added after "motive." The period bifurcating the thought, adding a punctual knockout, a tonal clobbering following thereafter from the facts of the matter, the fact of queer children killing themselves because this world does not know how to love them as they deserve to be loved. The harrowing heft of queer kids not making it, distributed.

5. THEORY FOR ALL

Judith Butler, author of *Gender Trouble* (1990), that North Star of queer theory that has been translated into many languages, first encountered Muñoz when he was a graduate student. The world-renowned queer theorist recounts: "I met him at Eve Sedgwick's home, if I remember correctly, and it seemed to me that he was, even then, gossiping, which is to say that he was very excited about knowing what people thought and felt, whom they loved, who has hurt them, and what comes next."[33] Young Muñoz, a graduate student, maybe in a turtleneck, sporting that lush head of curls, gossiping. I can't get the image out of my head—Muñoz lapping up the chisme in Sedgwick's living room. Perhaps he was in a corner of the room or on the edge of a couch, nursing a cocktail, the chisme too good to not indulge in, embracing a practice of queer Latinx communing, a source for the production of knowledge. Butler continues, "I eventually grasped that gossip was for him a form of sustained attention and investment made highly communicable, a contagious way of saying: 'Let's face it, we live through one another all the time.'"[34]

Can one gossip about the dead?

Do the dead have afterlives worthy of gossip?

In an online book forum in 2023, a user named seamus slattery, reviewing *Disidentifications*, provides a one-word assessment: "unbelievable." No stars are given.

I, too, love to gossip. Not as malice, nor ill-intentioned slander, but as a practice of speculating and hypothesizing with others upon the matter of things. Who might be sleeping with whom? How were this person's funds for their extravagant trip to Paris procured when they'd claimed on social media to be broke? When will a mutual see the light of day and leave their toxic partner, or stop their destructive behavior? Gossiping is a form of theorizing. We propose hypotheses on the matters at hand and determine if those theories bear any merit with respect to the facts we have at our disposal. We gossip to make sense of things. We gossip to gather knowledge. We gossip for pleasure.

Queers understand the value of gossip and its many purposes. We gather with those like us to engage in gossipy revelry in bars, living rooms, art galleries, parks, and bedrooms. Our gossiping produces knowledge of the world from a keenly queer perspective. Our gossiping takes up space when many would rather see us silenced or erased. Our gossiping is queer praxis. Our gossiping is a fabulously ordinary way of being, and thinking, together.

"The performativity of gossip thus enables an alternative version of community by disseminating alterative truths," writes Lee Edelman of Butler's anecdote on Muñoz gossiping.[35] Edelman sees Butler's analysis of Muñoz's gossiping as a reparative practice, in line with the theorizations on reparativity espoused by Muñoz's mentor, Eve Sedgwick. In this case, gossip becomes the relinquishing of all-knowingness and mastery, a practice of not ceding to a suspicious, paranoid position. Gossip excites a search for different forms of knowledge and community making, a humility in not quite knowing everything and being okay with it, spinning a yarn that allows for a little play in an all too frequently depressing reality. Gossip as philosophizing.

Something in common between the theorist and me: We're gossip queens.

Edelman, in the same essay that quotes Butler's reading of Muñoz's gossip, remarks upon a "tension" between the "type of queer theory I have come to represent (focused on irony, negativity, and the death drive) and the type of queer theory associated with the late José Esteban Muñoz (focused on community, social transformation, and the hope for a more inclusive future)."[36] It is easy to frame the two as oppositional thinkers, especially given how staunch a critique Muñoz mounts against Edelman in *Cruising Utopia*. However, Edelman reminds us that one's supposed orthodoxy to an approach is never as stable as one assumes. And that such supposed oppositional frameworks do not prohibit conviviality:

> On October 18, 2013, two months before he died, José and I chatted and reminisced with each other (there was probably some gossip, too) during a leisurely dinner in Somerville after a talk that he gave at Tufts. His lecture was drawn from material that would posthumously be published in *The Sense of Brown*. After talking about why I found his work in this project so compelling, especially insofar as it elaborated, far more fully than *Cruising Utopia*, the negativity on which the concept of disidentification

> rests, we spent several hours discussing the imbricated trajectories of our writing, and then passed on to recalling our adventures together when my partner, Joe, and I lived for a year in New York. We laughed at the recollection of a party that Joe and I held at our apartment where José passed the evening largely chatting with Eve, while his then-boyfriend seemed to do nothing more than hoover up refreshments. The dinner ended with our joint reconstruction of the night we all spent at Flamingo East seeing Kiki and Herb together. We promised, in parting, to keep in touch—would he be at January's MLA?—hugged each other and said goodbye. Two months later he died.[37]

This "remembrance," as Edelman calls it, is located in an endnote. For a queer theorist like him—who largely maintains an impersonal, critical distance and seriousness in his work—the endnote is the perfect place for the personal. His anecdote is also an example of that peculiar genre of storytelling: the recounting of the last time we saw someone before they died. We all do it. Remembering the final evening or day shared with the departed. The conversations had about one-off boyfriends or past dinners in New York City restaurants that don't exist anymore. The promises to keep in touch, the conferences that might be attended. There is something special about this genre of recounting the last time shared with the dead. It feels uniquely ours. We can share our moment with others who also knew the departed. Going around with our remembrances. Our memory a scar within us. One that we can't help but show others.

The adrenaline rush that accompanies gossip stems from the possibility that the gossiped-upon might find out about it, that the chisme might get back to them. It is the thrill of a potential confrontation that could be lighthearted or explosive, depending. Because the dead can't respond to gossip, there is none of the rush. Gossiping is for the living, it would seem.

. . . . . .

Other reader-reviewers in online forums praise *Disidentifications*, noting its importance in queer of color theory. Some lament the dryness of the writing, while others call it dense. But a number of reviewers call it accessible, in contrast to the work of other queer theorists like Sedgwick, Foucault, Butler. It all speaks to how readers can have wildly different experiences with the same theory. *Dense* operates as a pejorative, connotes writing—especially scholarly writing—that is difficult to parse quickly, demands attention, perhaps uses jargon. *Accessible* implies writing that is easy to understand, simple, straightforward, direct. Theory and critical reading have long been debated as being either accessible or inaccessible. Debates about the accessibility of particular works poke their heads up all the time from the halls of academia to the feeds of social media.

However, the call for accessible writing fails to account for how social and political transformation doesn't always happen within familiar, preestablished forms of knowing. Theory attempts to create a new sense of the world, and this is not always going to be expressible in the lexicons, syntax structures, and frameworks we have already been given. They must be invented, tested out, imagined. We will be challenged to unlearn, unthink, and think anew, differently.

Sometimes the expression of ideas, like everyday life, is messy, complicated, tricky, meaningfully polyvalent. Admittedly, the simply straightforward is nice to have when we can have it. Whether it be for the expression of ideas, or our relationships, or anything else in life, we sometimes need simplicity to maintain our well-being. However, simplicity most often does not even come close to defining the human experience. To demand that the communication of all thought and ideas be accessible fails to acknowledge the human condition, the wondrous complexity of the human mind. Some ideas require a multiclause sentence, others a simple sentence. Some ideas require jargon, or specific words that have a specific history and context, and others require no particular lexicon at all. Some ideas require specific modes and styles. When we take the time, when we meet the thought where it is, when we do the research to know how an idea developed, when we unthink what we have been taught is normal: This is how change happens. Difficulty, or being challenged, can initiate us into another sense of the world.

Muñoz's first published work, "The Heteroglossia of Queer Voices," is a 1992 review of an anthology on queer film criticism, *How Do I Look? Queer Film and Video*. The anthology had emerged out of a debate about academic style. Some of the essays that ended up in the anthology had initially been slated for publication in *October*, a scholarly journal specializing in contemporary criticism and theory, edited by Douglas Crimp. However, the editorial board ultimately overruled Crimp's plan and rejected the pieces because they were not felt to meet the journal's stylistic standards. Not theoretical enough. Crimp and the editorial collective behind the writings opted instead to publish them as an anthology with an independent press. Muñoz, who was still a graduate student at Duke at the time, observes in his review how the anthology "expands our understanding of what 'counts' as theory. Often the writers invent their own theoretical vernaculars that engage the cultural specificity of our diverse queer realities without compromising the powerful level of intellectual brilliance."[38] Even as a graduate student, Muñoz was already pressing his fellow academics to think more capaciously of what theory can be and feel like. Theory is not one thing, and the theoretical can take on many styles. It adapts to the theorist doing the theorizing. It cannot look the same from thinker to thinker, work to work, because contexts, people, and ideas change. The ways in which we articulate different ideas must change in order to meet the challenges of each idea. Nor, for that matter, can the reception of theory by audiences be uniform. We cannot expect a standard response from everyone. Theory will meet each reader where they are, and we in turn must meet it where we can, filling in the gaps along the way. In order to better understand a theory, we can undertake our own researches, zigzagging our own paths through knowledge. This is, I think, the beauty of theory: It pushes us to continue learning in order to better understand.

All of this is to say that theory requires us to have this understanding of its basic functions and history. For instance, the theorist you are reading does not think in a vacuum or generate wholly new ideas from thin air. There are lineages of thought (Marxism, deconstruction, aesthetic theory, Black feminist theory) after which one writes. One may not be able to read every theorist or book that came before in a particular lineage of thought, but it's important to know that ideas developed from one thinker to the next. Also, for example, theory examines the world using concepts and frameworks that ask us to step into the theorist's perspective. The critical toolbelt provided by the theorist is how we are to engage what they are theorizing about and then from there we can disagree or agree to our liking.

Call it an openness, if you will, but I suspect that theory asks for a critical receptivity to the unknown. It is about being receptive to what makes us uncomfortable, what challenges us, what leaves us bereft and behooved, transformed. Muñoz on punk rock music, a genre he loved, gets us to the heart of the matter: "the wildness of punk and its commons is that annihilative force, that refusal of cohesion and insistence on scatteredness, partiality, and the impossible act of not only living but also striving that are accomplished in an uncommon commons."[39]

As we've seen, capitalism also plays its part in structuring the material conditions in which we read theory. We get home at the end of the workday—or on the scant two-day weekend that many, but not all, get to claim for themselves—and are too beat up to do anything else besides scroll on our phones. I know this zombified feeling all too well. For that reason I sympathize with the demands for immediacy, simplicity, and directness that fly under the banner of the accessible. But this demand also reinforces various logics essential to capitalism's success: the offering up of the world as easy, seamless, uncomplicated. Capitalism has trained us to believe the world is our oyster. Capitalism robs ruthlessly, and one of the biggest robberies it has committed is our ability to provide attention. Being able to give extended and extensive attention to the world around us is a part of being human—it is a universal right. It is a practice needed to understand the intrinsic and unimpeachable worth of life of all kinds on this planet. Attention is the bread and butter of thoughtful and transformative analysis. We can't identify problems for what they are, nor dream up solutions, if we cannot pay adequate attention to how contexts, histories, and social forces unfold in the everyday. Capitalism necessitates that we not pay attention to the cruelties occurring all around us. Capitalism runs on us not seeing the exploitations happening right under our noses. To spot the system we need to notice it, all its cogs and gears, all its nuts and bolts, give a militant attention to its terrifying complexity.

Unbelievable. I can't parse seamus slattery's review. Unbelievable in a remarkable sense, a world-reorienting reading experience, or unbelievable in a disturbed sense, a waste of time?

Admittedly, I have no interest in punk rock. I don't know how to get into it, even when I tried to do so in order to better understand Muñoz's own fascination with the genre. The sound of it eludes me.

In the 1999 preface to the second edition of *Gender Trouble*, Judith Butler reflects on their book's surprising success: "It is no doubt strange, and maddening to some, to find a book that is not easily consumed to be 'popular' according to academic standards. The surprise over this is perhaps attributable to the way we underestimate the reading public, its capacity and desire for reading complicated and challenging texts, when the complication is not gratuitous, when the challenge is in the service of calling taken-for-granted truths into question, when the taken for grantedness of those truths is, indeed, oppressive."[40]

Some reader-reviewers note how the objects of study in *Disidentifications* are dated, or that these reader-reviewers don't necessarily know their context of emergence. Fair.

. . . . . .

Muñoz's posthumously published essay on the wildness of punk was intended to be part of a larger project on wildness, in collaboration with Jack Halberstam and Tavia Nyong'o. The two recall that the theorist had posed a question regarding the wild, and its potential relation to queer theory: "What if the 'queer' in queer theory were temporarily bracketed in order to examine everything that gathered under its sign and everything that remained beyond its purview?"[41] Wildness as a desired goal for the queer subject, wildness as a horizon for queerness itself. Another line of thought, another potential book, foreclosed.

In their introduction to a 1995 reader on the affect studies scholar Silvan Tomkins, Sedgwick, and Sedgwick's coeditor Adam Frank explain their fascination with the psychologist: "As people who fall in love with someone wish at the same time to exhibit themselves to others as *being loved*, we've also longed to do something we haven't been able to do more than begin here: to show how perfectly Tomkins understands *us*; to unveil a text spangled with unpathologizing, and at the same time unteleologizing, reflections on 'the depressive,' on claustrophilia, on the teacher's transference; on the rich life of everyday theories, and how expensively theories turn into Theory."[42]

As I read this passage, I mentally replace the name "Tomkins" with "Muñoz." Watch as the nominal substitution locks into place effortlessly, like in one of those Mad Libs I would do as a kid, where any answer-word would suffice to elicit a laugh. Speaking, as Tomkins did to Sedgwick and Frank, to what the theorist does for me, "how expensively theories turn into Theory." My word-doctoring an expression of what I do for love of theory.

Fantasy—like dating, like sex, like love—composes much of queer life, if not outright defining it. Fantasies of biological family that genuinely, unconditionally, care for us in all our fabulosity. Fantasies of friends who didn't prematurely die from disease or suicide or violence. Exes who worked out. Hookups who stayed regulars. Lives that got to be lived in their full queer splendor without restriction, repression, or compromise.

K'eguro Macharia sumptuously explicates: "Queers need fabulation. We need to imagine and theorize and practice strategies that make our beings possible. Against our training. For something else."[43]

Queers love fantasying. What could have been, what may be, what could still be, what will never be but, dammit, we deserve to imagine it. "Fantasy is the means by which people hoard idealizing theories and tableaux about how they and the world 'add up to something,'" notes queer theorist Lauren Berlant, another friend and contemporary of Muñoz.[44]

Queer life lavishes in the fantastic, darling.

Queer people have always had to deny their wishes and dreams in order to appease, or make peace, with the hostile world. History has so rarely done right by us. Fantasy slots itself almost seamlessly in the life of the queer person. It is ours, genuinely and unconditionally. We thrive in the subjunctive.

Barthes: "To unrealize: I refuse reality in the name of a fantasy. Everything around me changes value in relation to an imaginary. Example: someone who's in love unrealizes the world (which irritates him) with respect to the image of the loved one, which is his reality. In this sense, to unrealize the world is to realize the peripeteias and utopias of love."[45]

For Muñoz, the fantasies of queer life are a reality. He takes the fantasying work of queer people seriously enough that he becomes a scholar of it. Fantasy that is astoundingly real enough that his researches place queer people, particularly queers of color, from the "margins of other discourses to their very own discursive, emotional, and ideological center," as he wrote in 1995.[46] Fantasy gives life. Many lives, many shots at a different kind of life. Another entry-point in which to live, liberated.

. . . . . .

The theorist not yet fully a theorist writing his first book. I fantasize about having been there, in the process, the mind machinations, among the drafts and outlines, peeking over the shoulder and hearing the mumbled thoughts, those early stages, early states.

Being somehow magically present during this process of theory making and writing worlds, the book before it's a book—a frequent fantasy I have about many writers.

II

HE HAD TO HAVE . . .

There are few records proving that my queer Puerto Rican uncle ever existed. There is his obituary, which states that his death was caused by an unspecified illness. This was in 1991, two months before I was born, and as my childhood unfolded he was rarely spoken of. His mysterious illness, and what brought it about, went unmentioned. He was sequestered to a few old photos in my grandmother's house, on a side table or the hallway wall. It wasn't until I was a teenager that my mother told me what illness had taken him. I suppose she felt she *had* to say something, give a warning. She saw something in me that reminded her of him, her brother. Something she didn't like, something she thought that she could beat out of me. "AIDS killed your tío," she told me. The letters rang in my head. I had learned about AIDS in school, knew what it was: a gay disease, a disease that kills gays, a disease that gays brought about. AIDS was a gay disease and my gay Puerto Rican uncle had died from it.

My tío died as he lived: in obscurity. He came of age in the same New Jersey house where I would later grow up myself; he graduated high school in the late '70s and moved away, only to return sick nearly ten years later. No one in the family knew what he had been doing in his almost decade-long absence. But now he could no longer live on his own, as he must have told my grandparents on the day of his return. According to my mother, he only told my grandparents, my mother, and his four other brothers that he had AIDS. There would be no more discussion of it by the immediate family. My maternal grandparents attempted to keep the highly stigmatized disease hidden. But of course the extended family quickly found out—it was impossible to hide. These family members stopped coming to my grandparents' house, fearful as they were of the gay disease, scared to touch pillows, to put a spoon in the mouth, to breathe the same air that my tío breathed. His purple Kaposi sarcoma lesions spread, he grew terribly frail, and in the later stages he lost his vision. He died in the family home, in a room I never I really liked. Shortly thereafter, his brother would come to reside in that room, after his divorce.

To this day, no one in my family seems to know who his lovers or friends had been before he got sick. No one knows what establishments he frequented, what he cooked himself for dinner, what he liked to do on the weekends. There are no photos of my uncle while living an out, queer life in the '80s. No letters, no diaries, no trace of what his life was like before AIDS.

He was young, and then he was dying. This is the record.

"Ephemera as Evidence" is one of Muñoz's earliest articles. Published in 1996 as the introduction to a special issue of the journal *Women & Performance*, the short piece functions as an intervention into scholarly protocol and methodology. In it, Muñoz called for theorists to reconsider what can be taken as proof, or evidence, when theorizing queer life. Conventional scholarly practice and legitimacy hinged upon a concrete archive to be studied: a written text, a testimony, a film, an artwork. An object that could be materialized for another to see for oneself. At the time that this piece was published, at the height of the AIDS epidemic, before viable treatment was available, queer life seemed dangerously ephemeral. Moreover, for those who were expecting to pass, the most pressing matter was not always planning for what would happen to the material evidence of their lives. Muñoz therefore argued that ephemera and performance—those things that exist in a moment and typically go undocumented—are valid evidence of queer worldmaking practices: "those things that remain after a performance, a kind of evidence of what has transpired but certainly not the thing itself" that "follow[s] traces, glimmers, residues, and specks of things."[1] The way a body moved in a club, the sound of the voice in the microphone, the way one person glanced at another. This ephemeral methodology, Muñoz emphasized, is deployed by minoritized critics and cultures in order to presence what otherwise gets brushed aside as unverifiable, illegitimate, and unworthy. If we take ephemera seriously, we can discern within it queer pasts, presents, and futures.

Muñoz frames his conceptualizing of the ephemeral through what he terms "the tyranny of identity," writing that we must move beyond overdetermined, preestablished identity essentialisms. This anti-identitarian politic is a vitally important theoretical force and through line in all of Muñoz's work. This is not to say that he sees such identities as unimportant in establishing a sense of self, community, or aesthetic practice, or that identity can be written off as inconsequential when considering how we move through the world. Rather, an anti-identitarian approach critiques reductive identity formations, which only serve to foreclose possibilities for enacting radical transformation. We all, no matter our individual identities, have the ability to effect change for seemingly different, and competing, political agendas and causes. This is why queer acts, or the power of doing, rather than merely meaning or just being, he proposes, is a better foundation for queer worldmaking. "'Performativity' is already quite a queer category," Sedgwick had avowed in 1991.[2] Performance operationalizes another sense of the world right then and there, in the act of doing.

Before my tío arrived at my grandparents' house to tell them he was terminally ill, he had to have danced. To Madonna, I'm sure—"Into the Groove" and "Material Girl" were enormous hits during his first years away from home, his prime clubbing years. Maybe, on one of those nights, Janet's "When I Think of You" was on and he was getting messy, feeling himself, though his dancing was okay; in his feelings and in his body was all that mattered. On a special night like Latin night, the queer clubs had to have played Eddie Santiago's 1986 salsa hits, "Que Locura Enamorarme de Ti" or "Tú Me Quemas," and he would have been shaking those hips, thinking of the Puerto Rican family he left behind, of islands and barrios as he twisted and turned with another man, or with girlfriends who celebrated his salsero femininity.

Or maybe Rick Astley's 1987 "Never Gonna Give You Up" was his jam, was one of the last club hits he would dance to before he got a little too sick to stand, before seizures incapacitated him, before he died from—as his obituary identified in secret, yet open, shame—"his illness." Who knows. It was the '80s.

He had to have touched other men in those crowded nightclubs. Kissed one, kissed many. Drink in hand, gin and tonic sloshing, sticky hands on sweaty bodies. He was stick-thin, unlike me, had to have been more malleable, bending over the arm of a lover. He had to have desired and lusted over other queer bodies, though none of my family knows these details, none wanted to know because they couldn't handle the fact that their own little macho yearned for boy dicks and boy asses, yearned to fuck dangerously, to fuck until the end of days.

He had to have fucked in the club. On the floor of the bathroom. On a pool table in the back of a sleazy bar. He wouldn't have minded a little dirt and grime. Wasn't that upscale kinda gay. Was he even gay? My mother speculates he was bisexual; when he returned to my grandparents' home, too sick to care for himself, she remembers him reaching out to women to let them know of his status. Who knows, really, but I know he wasn't an upper-crust kinda queer.

He must have liked to fuck and get fucked. Maybe he liked blowing men in Central Park, liked eating ass on the piers with Jersey on the horizon. He had to have been a slut. Must have been proud of it, too, and all who knew him knew him to be so. But who did know him? Who can claim knowledge of his life during those years he was his full queer self? My tío, who lived with and died of AIDS. My tío, who took to his grave his years in the '80s, his years being wild and deviant, his years loving and fucking and caring for others like him.

What do I know? I can only speculate upon a past I will never know, a history I concoct through the details of past queer lives I've heard about. An archive of my imagination.

I like how Muñoz conceptualizes ephemera at the smallest scale: They are "traces, glimmers, residues, and specks of things." They are quaint, nearly unnoticeable, like dust in sunbeams, perfume on clothes from departed loved ones, a new ingredient added to a favorite dish. In his second book, *Cruising Utopia*—published in 2009, almost fifteen years after "Ephemera as Evidence"—Muñoz further elaborates upon his thinking on the ephemeral:

> Ephemera are the remains that are often embedded in queer acts, in both stories we tell one another and communicative physical gestures such as the cool look of a street cruise, a lingering handshake between recent acquaintances, or the mannish strut of a particularly confident woman.[3]

These queer acts are hardly given expression out loud but are militantly observed by queers, instrumental in evidencing queer life, history, and relationality. These traces of queerness keep us going, honey. They demand fine-grain noticing: close attention as a method of care on behalf of queer life. The minor registers a place to linger in, and account for, what has been erased.

Admittedly, it gets exhausting thinking about how to combat erasure. For queer people of color, erasure has defined our collective histories. We have had to fight tooth and nail to recover ourselves in historical narratives that have erased our queerness, or our color, or both at the same time. I think about it when I don't necessarily even want to think about it. Sitting at home over dinner, or at a bar sipping a cocktail, stewing in queer rage over what was, or what could have been, pointing out pain and injustice on a Monday night or an early Friday evening, not exactly sure what to do with the feelings.

I get into these tailspins often. Feel a righteousness that I'm never entirely sure what to do with. My boyfriend listens attentively to my qualms, validates what I'm saying. There's nothing exactly for you to do, he says, which makes me feel both calmer and more horrible. No time machine to return to the past and change events. No way to know for sure how things were for those that came before us. The timelines are over, the stories and details of lives dimly remembered, the names forgotten. If they were ever remembered to begin with. Why does the queer past weigh so heavily on me? How do I reconcile with the pain and violences of yesterday? Nothing to do, exactly, but I still need to pursue the doing. I do my somethings. My reimaginings, my retellings. The possible futility of the effort matters.

"love can / bust you up in increments so," go the lines of a poem entitled "josé muñoz," an ode to the queer of color theorist, written by his friend and colleague Fred Moten and published in 2010, when the theorist was still living.[4] It is a rare—and, to my knowledge, the only—piece of writing to honor the theorist in his lifetime, before the deluge of commemorative writings, arts, and events that emerged posthumously. Moten gives voice to the theorist in the opening lines, marked by a present-tense liveliness: "I love my students (why / is this a performative? I am I do what / ever I say I do I am if I," while also serving up a side of on-the-nose humor about Muñoz being a performance studies scholar. One can sense the love of friendship radiating throughout the lines, that knowing depth. "you link ephemera / substitute beautify," concludes the poem. Concepts enshrined in poetic form, queer theory made cheeky lyric. A poem fit for a theorist.

......

My boyfriend pointed out to me one day how one of the people in *Paris Is Burning* looks exactly like my uncle. He was right. The resemblance is uncanny. The bony body, the slim face, the long wavy hair, and the light skin. Is it actually him? Was he there in Harlem, vogueing through the ball circuits, snapping his fingers in applause? I can't be sure. I don't know if I will ever be sure.

I don't know how the person in the film identified in terms of their gender back then. I don't know how they identify now—if there is even a now for a queer body of color like that one. They appear in the first three minutes of the film in striped gray overalls and an orange shirt, voguing before Madonna made it cool, knees bending into angularity and arms flinging outward. A few seconds later is a close-up shot of the person. They have won a category and are holding their trophy in their hands, stretching theatrically to be seen. Their hair is a lengthily wavy opulence. They are Puerto Rican, no doubt about it. One of those thousands upon thousands who migrated to the mainland, to New York City, New Jersey, Connecticut. Full of dreams, yet dream-denied.

Look at me, their body says to the camera, *look at me*. Posing for the crowd around them, for the camera in front of them, for the viewer who will watch the film in the '90s, the 2000s, the 2010s, and beyond. They're a winner, baby, and they want us to know it—that imagined *us*, extended across space and time. After holding the pose for a few seconds, they give a slight smile. Coyness in the upturn. They know something we don't. What is it, girl? What knowledge do you have that transcends your time, my time, all time? Tell us about the queer timeless. Tell us about queer eternity. How do we get there?

I rewatch the documentary for what seems to be the fifteenth time. I must scope out this body again. Pausing, rewinding, pausing, fast-forwarding. I keep pausing on their image. zooming in. My own homemade close-ups. Film scholar Mary Ann Doane describes close-ups of human faces as "a critical breakdown in the opposition between subject and object"[5] that "provokes a sense of the tangible, the intimate."[6] For Doane, the close-up conducts an "annihilation of a sense of depth and its corresponding rules of perspectival realism" where "the world is reduced to this face, this image."[7] This works to close the gulf between viewer and object, generating a sense of cinematic intimacy and scrutiny.

The person appears in several more shots throughout the documentary. In one, they are kneeling over huddled with a group of queers in the ballroom. They chew gum furiously—gum-chewing a femme aesthetic, an art form. In another shot, they are applauding enthusiastically for a queen vogueing down the runway. There are other quick glimpses. In each shot, they are always in the periphery. We never hear them speak. They have no name in the credits. They are given no story within the film. But they are not alone in that regard. Think of all other Black and brown bodies moving in and out of the documentary. The filmic flashes of unidentified bodies back-bending expertly, snapping fingers in approval of a performer, laughing riotously at a joke we will never know. All these bodies telling stories in gesture, in poses, in countenance. All these body stories if we pay them a little more attention.

In *Disidentifications*, Muñoz maintains that *Paris Is Burning* primarily glamorizes queer and trans of color pain, disease, and poverty. That the director, Jennie Livingston, makes a spectacle of the ball-goers at the expense of a more nuanced, critical understanding of their lives. His argument joins those of many other scholars and critics who are skeptical of the film, of the white filmmaker, of the way she presents her documentary subjects. In his later writing, though, Muñoz qualifies his criticism of the film, noting that "queers watched *Paris Is Burning* because it promised a world, glimmering and glamorous, tinged with criminality and discord, haunted with the specter of tragedy. So many learned the word 'shade,' as in 'throwing shade,' from that film, and while that phrase is not new, its descriptive force has not waned when discussing contemporary queer of color life."[8] I agree with Muñoz's reappraisal of the film. *Paris Is*

Burning is a crucial document of queer and trans of color life. There are so few like it. It provides insight into queer and trans life in 1980s New York, into the voices and lexicons of the culture. It has opened up opportunities for all kinds of audiences to learn about queer and trans of color life from the past. It is a gateway, I believe, and one that demands more critical frameworks and approaches to understanding the subjects and histories it depicts. We need to look closer, imagine more broadly, connect in the ways we can.

"you link ephemera / substitute beautify"

Lauren Berlant: "I do not read things; I read with things. When I read with theorists, with art, with a colleague or friend, *to read with* is to cultivate a quality of attention to the disturbance of their alien epistemology, an experience of nonsovereignty that shakes my confidence in a way from which I have learned to derive pleasure, induce attachment, and maintain curiosity about the enigmas and insecurities that I can also barely stand or comprehend."[9]

In 2014, Manhattan's La MaMa Galleria, in collaboration with the community-based organization Visual AIDS, hosted a multi-artist exhibition titled "Ephemera as Evidence," inspired by Muñoz's essay of the same name. Curators Joshua Lubin-Levy and Ricardo Montez wrote in the show's catalog that they consider "thinking through the ephemeral as necessary to the political life of HIV. . . . The exhibition acknowledges a larger history of silence and erasure while at the same time making salient strategies for survival and worldmaking potentials in the face of a violently phobic public sphere."[10] The artists and performers represented in the exhibition—several of whom were friends and collaborators of Muñoz, including Nao Bustamante, Tony Just, Kevin McCarty, and D-L Alvarez—grappled with the notion of the ephemeral and its relation to the past, present, and future of HIV/AIDS. *Sustaining Ephemeralities (on the Dole)* (2014), by the filmmaker and AIDS activist James Wentzy, was a pile of empty pill bottles that once contained protease inhibitors, known colloquially as the "cocktail." The disposed bottles showed how the drugs have allowed HIV-positive positive life to continue, how they have affirmed queer life itself as still viable. Yet they also spoke to the systematic disposability of queers and the sick. Hugh Steers's painting, *Chair to Bed* (1993), showed a muscular, masculine figure holding onto the end of a bedrail with one hand as they slip out of a white garment, a pair of black high heels still on their feet. A man seated in an armchair holds their other hand. Is this a drag entertainer returning home to a helpful partner? A cross-dressing sexual tryst? Whatever the scenario may be, the painting documents a scene of disappearance: the slipping out of one identity into another, dressed to undressed, drag performer to sexual partner, worker to lover—or, maybe, the worker-lover paid to be there, readying themselves for sleep or sex. The painting spotlights the kind of forgettable, yet ordinary, instances of transition that we all perform, in some capacity or another.

The exhibition highlighted how HIV/AIDS made the ephemeral political. It showed that all those queers who never got to see their twenties, their thirties, their forties, they mattered. No matter how short their lives may have been, they mattered. No matter how devastatingly brief a queer neighborhood's or community's existence may have been, it mattered. No matter how little materially was left behind, it all mattered. The ephemeral became a place in which to think, organize, and demand radical transformation on behalf of queer life. The gone-too-soon, the fleeting, the without-a-trace, the transitional, the lacking-history all came to matter because we needed it to. Queer life has persisted against all the odds, has endured through the thinnest of margins. Queers have lasted because we have been a crafty, cunning bunch, from generation to generation, always improvising and readapting, doing the best we can with what little we got.

......

Jean-Luc Nancy, a French theorist of immense importance to Muñoz, wrote a poem called "Ode to José Esteban Muñoz" in 2014, one year after his death. The poem was published in a special issue of the journal *Social Text*, where Muñoz had been an editor. The issue, dedicated to Muñoz, assembles memorials from friends and colleagues, a beautiful tribute to the impact of his work and life. "So where are you, José Esteban? in the *socio* or in the *patho*?" queries the narrator in Nancy's ode.[11] Like Moten's ode, Nancy's integrates Muñoz's concepts and theories, evoking them in a whimsical tone. "where have you gone to disidentify? Where, tell us!" Wherever the theorist has gone, Nancy writes, "all that matters is that you are there." In that elsewhere, the theories dreamed up on Earth become total reality. No longer words on the page, no longer lectures at the lectern, no longer attempts or strategies or minor successes, but actual, realized after the point of vanishing.

I want so much to see my tío in *Paris Is Burning*. I want to see him alive, in movement—chewing gum, smoking a cigarette, getting himself ready to pose for the camera. I want to see him joyous. I want to know that queer inheritance does not have to be only suffering and pain. I need to believe there was also pleasure in our pasts. That I have inherited raucous and wild ways of being with other queers. My watching is bent only on seeing this queer body that resembles my tío. To see him doing those things that no one in our family seemed to able to imagine. Yet, as committed as I am to seeing what I want to see, my attention wanders to other queer bodies on the screen.

I notice the way the camera focuses on a young unidentified Black body, lean and limber and lounging on a couch. At the same time, Pepper LaBeija, blurred and out of focus, talks of how young queers are being kicked out of their homes and are coming to him for a mother/father figure. We are clearly meant to be listening to Pepper, but the camera gears our line of sight to the lounging body lying there, divinely at ease as they are.

Halfway through the film, there is a shot outside a dance hall of two very young queers, one from Harlem and one from the Bronx, both definitely Puerto Rican. The one from Harlem speaks to the camera about queer family and what it means to choose one's family. While philosophizing, the one from Harlem playfully rests their shoulder on the queer from the Bronx. Their hand, eventually, slides down the white tank top of their Bronx companion, gently, slowly, affectionately. Hickies appear to be on both of their necks. Are they lovers? The hand sliding down the chest, not holding, not grasping, merely wanting to touch, to let the other know that *I will love you though your blood kin might not, though we might not make it to tomorrow, will love you beyond the '80s, beyond New York, beyond time and space.*

These moments are little bursts of queer joy and pleasure. So brief, so fleeting, so banal. Yet they hit me to my core. They remind me of what being queer is all about. That it's about the lounging on a couch with those you choose to call family. That it's about a hand gently moving across a chest while on the street, flaunting hickies, for all to see. That it's about the remarkably unremarkable lives we live and have lived and will live.

The strokes of fingers through black and tan paint. Zigzagging around, forming no representative image, aiming aimlessly. Sloppy, grimy doodles on canvas. The technique reminds me of when the oil from our family cars would leak onto the pavement, oozing into the nearby mud caked around the fenceposts, tar black mixing with muddy dark brown. I'd stick my index finger in the goop, scrawling nonsense on the sidewalk. Just passing time, killing suburban boredom. The non-artwork wiped away within a few hours by the boots of men leveling the strokes, or the barrage of a summer shower, or my grandmother hosing down the area. There one moment, gone the next.

Tony Just's oil painting *Untitled* (2007) was included in "Ephemera as Evidence." The finger strokes are in the topmost section. In other parts of the canvas are thinner scratches, as if done by the edge of a fingernail, forming jagged curves and rough lines. The various types of strokes across the canvas look as if they could be wiped away easily, if desired. The texture also lures us to smudge it further with our own bodily strokes. Adding on and taking away, erasing and presencing, a goopy looping with no discernible start or finish. Muñoz wrote that Tony Just's work is "emblematic of the kind of invisible evidence" constituting ephemera.[12] We know it's there, those traces that most certainly belong to a finger or nail, those doodled smudges doing something inexpressibly expressible. We know it—whatever that *it* precisely is—to be true. Call it a hunch, call it queerness's long durée.

I am no longer angry at my family for what they did to my uncle. I don't forgive them, however, and I don't forget. Their shame was a violence. Their embarrassment the perpetuation of stigma. Their choices the suppression of a queer life they knew and called family. Their erasure of him resounds today, in my life. The record of my uncle gone, and it feels like there is no viable path to reclaiming what has been lost. What bits I have, I make do with. I look for him in unidentified strangers in a documentary. I pause, I magnify, I pan out, I screenshot. Technology extending the life snuffed out by disease, familial shame, and governmental neglect. I search for a queer ancestor in the nooks and crannies of archives, histories forgotten. Though I am not religious, uncertain about an afterlife, I hope, somewhere, that my tío who never got to be my tío finds comfort in my wayward researches. My private devotions to his queer personhood. I hope he knows that I think of his queerness as something precious and divine. I hope he knows I loved him for being the queer no one else wanted to remember him being. I hope he knows that when I think of him I think of miracles, that despite all the odds, despite all the erasures, despite us never getting to cross paths on this Earth, I have come to know him. I hope he knows that I never gave up on imagining him living a queer life.

. . . . . .

Muñoz: "The work of queer inquiry is not simply to celebrate the lives and works of exemplary gays and lesbians, but instead to attend to the animating force of queer energies that saturate various cultural sites that may or may not be attached to queer biographies or even experiences."[13]

Imagine it. Another timeline. One where he had lived through 1991, had lived to see me born.

Had he been there, he would have taught me to dance in my grandparents' living room. He would have taught me salsa when no one was looking because he wanted to show me how to swish my hips, how to bend my body, how to pose. He would have taken me out for my first time at the queer club, let me sip on his drink, told me the chisme of the men he slept with. My tío would have traveled the world tasting the flesh of strangers, and would have always returned to tell me about it.

Had he lived, he would have sat with my family and told them how he forgave them for avoiding the house, for not wanting to put their lips on the well-washed knives and forks and plates and cups, for writing up that obituary that erased his cause of death.

But that is not my timeline. Mine is this one. This imagined past is not mine and will never be anyone's, because it is all speculation, a collage of details from documentaries, literature, and anecdotes told by the queer elders I have been fortunate enough to know. All I can do is imagine that he had to have danced. He had to have touched another man. He had to have fucked in the club. He had to have lived, once upon a time, my tío, in a nightclub, on the corner of the street, in a dimly lit bathroom, feeling his body free, loose and limber, touching and being touched, so wondrously alive.

III

IN THE OFFICE WITH YOU

More than a decade after his death, Muñoz's faculty page is still up on NYU's website. It lists his former office address, 721 Broadway, 6FL, marking an absence that is now someone else's presence. Office space in downtown Manhattan, where NYU is located, is too expensive to let the fear of a haunting keep space unused. The website also lists his research interests: "Latino studies; queer theory; critical race theory; global mass cultures; performance art; film and video." The catchwords seem too simple, too reductive, to speak to the nature of his expansive, unsummarizable theorizing. His email in the corner of the page: jose.munoz@nyu.edu. A lure for epistolary desiring. Cold emails beyond the grave.

Answering the question "What is performance studies?" in a 2002 interview with performance studies scholar Diana Taylor, Muñoz replies, "When I was in graduate school, I was in a literature program. It was very epistemologically heavy. All about what we know about a text or the infinite play of interpretation. There's a thing about performance studies that is very useful to me because it's more about what a text does."[1] This is one of the few video recordings of Muñoz available to the public. Most of them are lectures, presentations of his research in progress. They are filmed hazily, at a distance, Muñoz behind a lectern or table. The interview with Taylor is different, undertaken in what appears to be his NYU office, a shelf of books as backdrop, the camera closely cropped on his face, no obstructing lectern or table. He sounds nervous, his *uhms* punctuating every other second of the six-minute video. The *uhms* are in the lecture recordings, too. Signature of his style? Indications not of nerves but of thought. A performative repetition where thinking happens. A world of thought unfolding, finding formation, lips vibrating out an idea.

I rewatch the video several times. The *uhms* have an entrancing effect, the sonic percolating of Muñoz across my eardrums. This mediated intimacy all I will know of him.

If I sent a message to the listed email, would anyone reply?

In 2009, Muñoz published his now widely read and cited second book, *Cruising Utopia: The Then and There of Queer Futurity*. Similar to *Disidentifications*, the book is a compilation of short chapters. The chapters theorize upon queer utopianism, with Muñoz examining various performers and artists like Frank O'Hara, Amiri Baraka, Kevin Aviance, and Andy Warhol. In these performers' various utopic enactments, Muñoz identifies glimmers of queer hope that shine a spotlight on another configuration of the world. The now-famous refrain opens the book: "Queerness is not yet here. Queerness is an ideality. Put another way, we are not yet queer."[2] Muñoz's ideas on utopianism set themselves against the stifling pragmatism of the mainstream LGBTQ movements that have equated queer rights with inclusion in oppressive heteronormative structures, rather than their dismantling. The Human Rights Campaign is emblematic of such a pragmatic positioning. Muñoz's book also positions itself against the anti-relational thesis then being championed by theorists like Lee Edelman and Leo Bersani. Influenced by psychoanalytic thought, the anti-relational thesis proclaimed the death drive, and a rejection of reproductive futurity that attaches itself to straight time, as strategies for queer critique. It asserted that queer practice and life should reject the heteronormative structures handed down to us—that is, the nuclear, reproducing family unit and the Child who represents futurity—and instead embrace a queer negativity (that is, queer pleasure and individuality above all else). Anti-relational analysis also criticized utopian thinking as vapid idealism at best, and as an apolitical optimism at worst.

Muñoz staunchly maintained that the anti-relational thesis relied upon distancing queerness from race, gender, nationality, and other vectors of social difference, all in service of upholding sexuality as the preeminent difference that superseded all others. He wrote: "I have been of the opinion that antirelational approaches to queer theory were wishful thinking, investments in deferring various dreams of difference. It has been clear to many of us, for quite a while now, that the antirelational in queer studies was the gay white man's last stand."[3] Queer of color theory's intervention into critical thought would ensure that the intersections of race, sexuality, and gender could not be overlooked any longer. He clarified in an endnote: "I do not mean all gay white men in queer studies. More precisely, I am referring to gay white male scholars who imagine sexuality as a discrete category that can be abstracted and isolated from other antagonisms in the social, which include race and gender."[4] This pattern continues today—whether in queer academia or in the general culture, white folks try to make sexuality or gender identity discrete from, and uncontaminated by, other axes of social difference. Race particularly complicates any straightforward, streamlined notion of sexuality or gender identity.

Following German philosopher Ernst Bloch's theorizations on abstract and concrete utopias—abstract utopias as wishful thinking without any will to change and concrete utopias wishful thinking with the will to change, which is where hope lies—Muñoz asserted that "A queer utopian hermeneutic would thus be queer in its aim to look for queer relational formations within the social," activated by "not settling for the present, of asking and looking beyond the here and now."[5] Muñoz postulates queer utopianism as a forward-looking, anticipatory horizon, allowing us to envision something we do not yet know or fully perceive. This is what utopian thinking offers. Blueprints for a queer world not yet here emerge in the ephemeral: in the glimpses, gestures, and other quotidian acts that harbor potential to reengage the past for a different future. For Muñoz, utopianism and hope are valuable tools for collective action and political mobilization, especially for queers of color. *Cruising Utopia* establishes utopianism as a viable queer politic, a radicalization of hope and futurity that is not apolitical or sentimental, offering us another sense of the world that is shot through with potentiality yet to be realized. We just have to work for it.

The theorist's interest in utopianism did not begin with *Cruising Utopia*. He concluded 1996's "Ephemera as Evidence" by mentioning how "Foucault's investigations into a time and place before the regime of identity is propelled by a longing for a utopia figured in the past that critiques the present."[6] And in his first book he remarked, "Disidentificatory performances and readings require an active kernel of utopian possibility." And: "Although utopianism has become the bad object of much contemporary political thinking, we nonetheless need to hold on to and even *risk* utopianism if we are to engage in the labor of making a queerworld."[7] And in a 2002 meditation on teaching in the aftermath of 9/11, we read: "Teaching itself can be thought of as the performance of utopia."[8]

Cruising Utopia is, by far, Muñoz's most widely read book. It achieved the crossover so many theoretical books strive for. The book made a name for itself in a world chock-full of anti-intellectualism. On Goodreads there are over one thousand ratings, and over one hundred written reviews. Not too shabby for a book of queer theory (Jack Halberstam's *The Queer of Art Failure* has over two thousand ratings, which feels monumental). *Publishers Weekly*, which does not frequently cover scholarly monographs, reviewed the book positively, albeit with a concluding barb not unfamiliar to other theoreticians who get broader press: "Queer theorists will find the book's provocative thesis stimulating; lay readers unfamiliar with Ernst Bloch and the Frankfurt School of philosophy on which the author builds his argument may find it a slog."[9] *Cruising Utopia* is not only vociferously referenced in scholarly journals and monographs across a range of disciplines but also in venues like the *New York Times*, *The Atlantic*, and the *Boston Review*. On TikTok, creators provide fast-paced video summarizations of the book—theoretical sound bites that address a younger crowd of possible future readers of queer theory. The queer of color theorist's ideas seem only to proliferate.

The italics in "*risk* utopianism"—in my head I hear the theorist say it with emphasis, a hand clenched. The enunciative force of the italicized proposition made audible.

I read *Cruising Utopia* as a doctoral student. My theory chops were much more fine-tuned than they had been when I first encountered *Disidentifications*. The sentences and terms imprinted more readily on my mind, and I moved through the book much more easily. Yet the encounter was still a revelation. I was stupefied from beginning to end. Highlighting with reckless abandon, as I had with other monographs by Muñoz and other theorists that had taken me time and rereading to understand. My first copy of *Cruising Utopia* is unreadable to my mature sensibilities.

I had never before thought of utopianism—or, more accurately, had not thought of the concept of the utopian proper, and its historical-theoretical lineage—before reading Muñoz. The perfect society where everyone is equal and all is fair was an idea I had only ever seen in novels and films (*The Giver*, read in a high school English class; *Demolition Man*, taking the concept to comedic extremes), often torqued to dystopic ends. Dystopia is never far off, it seems.

The epigraph to *Cruising Utopia* is a quote from Oscar Wilde, a name I was more familiar with than any theory on the utopian: "A map of the world that does not include utopia is not worth glancing at." I'd never read that particular line until I encountered it in Muñoz, but I had gone through a significant amount of Wilde's literary corpus already. Wilde, to me, was a tragic figure, a victim of a British empire defining homosexuality in order to pass laws against it by banning sodomy. He, the first legal homosexual, was made an example of by that law, which in the end cost him his freedom. "There are times when Sorrow seems to me to be the only truth," wrote Wilde to his former lover, Bosie, during his imprisonment between the years 1895 and 1897. He was sentenced to hard labor. "Other things may be illusions of the eye or the appetite, made to blind the one and cloy the other, but out of Sorrow have the worlds been built, and at the birth of a child or a star there is pain."[10] Wilde's letter to Bosie, which would come to be known as "De Profundis," gives a portrait of a man defeated. Carcerality kills the soul, kills the utopian impulse. That is, after all, what prisons are designed to do: kill the hope in imagining another world. But between the lines of Wilde's tonally defeated, surveilled letters to Bosie (for he knew his letters were being watched, that the public would sooner or later get their hands on them), he offers a glimmer beyond the stultifying grief: "*There are times* when Sorrow *seems to me* to be the only truth." (emphasis added)

If *there are times* of sorrow, then that means there are also times for joy, pleasure, euphoria, rage.

If it *seems* that sorrow is the only truth in certain moments, that means that the seeming can morph into something else. What seems to be doesn't have to be.

The pain of sorrow—which, for Wilde, is the violence of the carceral state against queer people—does not have to be total. We can follow the critic D. A. Miller in his treatise on Roland Barthes's gay sensibility; we can "notice and articulate" the queer signals that otherwise get suppressed.[11] These moments, in Wilde's letter to Bosie, are the queer utopic pulling through. Syntactical insurgencies against a state watching him for the slightest queer indiscretion. Wilde would die not too shortly after he was freed from prison, ground down by poverty and illness. "Hope's biggest obstacle is failure," declares Muñoz in a posthumously published lecture, "Hope in the Face of Heartbreak."[12] Society failed Wilde. His talent and vivacity were trampled upon by a world that saw in him something that needed to be eliminated. That malicious force is, always and ever, crushing, a reality that, far too frequently, causes the best of us to find ways to quit this earth in hopes of finding something better. And that is what happened to Wilde in many ways. He couldn't go on in a world so cruel and awful. His utopia wasn't here. Still not yet here. But he gave us some coordinates to scope out. Showed us some ways to glimpse that map yet to exist.

Cruising Utopia came out ten years after *Disidentifications*. Muñoz's thinking is more streamlined in the later book, his theoretical through line more unified. Queerness is the modus operandi. Critical commentary on *Cruising Utopia* and its legacy notes how it has become the most popular (and cited) of Muñoz's texts primarily because it emphasizes queerness over other axes of social difference, especially race. Whereas *Disidentifications* makes starkly clear in every chapter that the analytic framework is queer and non-white, its goal one more of critique rather than reparation, *Cruising Utopia* focuses more on queerness. And, of course, its theme of utopianism—the hope for a perfect society that yet can be—lends itself to positive reads.

One must read between the lines in order to detect the deeper implications of *Cruising Utopia*'s relative popularity over *Disidentifications*: white people find *Cruising Utopia* more comfortably applicable, and adoptable, for their needs. If a text marks race, it then becomes something that white queer people either distance themselves from or declare their inability to identify with. And if a text marks queerness as a non-white phenomenon, it becomes "niche." Of course, Muñoz does in fact mark race in *Cruising Utopia*, noting whether the cultural producers he is analyzing are white or non-white. Race is always of intellectual interest to Muñoz. Nevertheless, *Cruising Utopia* has been read in ways that purposefully overlook race.

A word I've heard often in academia and publishing: *niche*. Queer and trans of color art, culture, and life, as the refrain goes, are too niche for a broader audience to understand or want to engage with. Too specific, too particular, too small a group, and therefore unworthy of attention, funding, resources. Imagine if we tried to refine the category of queer and trans of color even further—if we tried to think of or advocate for queer Mexican American identity, or trans Vietnamese American identity. The niche only gets more niche!

A reader's need to identify with a text is a natural impulse, especially for marginalized folks. In recent years, nurturing such connections has been the charge of many Diversity, Equity, and Inclusion initiatives, which often spearhead programs to help children and adults find texts in which they can see themselves. A robust language has developed around this type of advocacy: "representation matters," "feeling seen," "inclusion." These are important and necessary, yet the pursuit of the relatable poses its own challenges. It is no wonder, then, that in a cultural landscape like the United States, where white people lead in positions of power and call the shots as to whose projects get funded, that minoritized groups become "niche." What is relatable to those who hold power becomes the unspoken universal standard, such that they don't perceive that their identity is one among many, like the rest of us.

But there are no niche groups other than the ones that those in power create. All art is universal. All art is for everyone to experience. The problem is that some art challenges, discomfits, and forces critical reflection of society's dominant groups (white, male, able-bodied, cisgender, heterosexual, monied). For dominant-group readers, these works do not produce the feel-good response of relatability. There is little to no critical language available in which to articulate a reading response of unrelatability. Most readers don't know how to respond to the unfamiliar, the discomfiting, the unrelatable, the not-same. This is especially true for those who belong to any of the dominant identity categories like white, male, cisgender, heterosexual, or able-bodied. Such responses play out most evidently in book bans that transpire not only in the United States but globally. Books by authors of color get banned. Books by queer and trans authors get banned. When dominant groups feel threatened, when they cannot relate, when they feel challenged in some way, they respond with hostility. Book banning is an extreme form of what happens when people in a dominant group cannot relate to a cultural object from a minoritized group. We see how various other expressions of unrelating manifest in underfunding various voices and communities, in overlooking various voices and communities for awards and recognitions, and in the complete lack of regard for them. These are sanctioned forms of ostracization, legitimate and culturally acceptable ways we keep "unrelatable" art and people in their place.

What would happen if, instead, our educational institutions and popular culture equipped us with the critical tools necessary to respond productively to social differences? If we were taught to honor experiences that are not like ours and don't need to be ours, to meet the discomfiting and the unfamiliar with curiosity and eagerness, to not fear learning, growing, perhaps even changing? Humans, especially those who benefit from the current structures in some way, are desperately fearful of change. This is why encountering art that centers the differences of others is met with hostility. Change is scary. Change may be desired but one does not how to go about it. A world not quite like this one is a notion too unthinkable for the majority of this overheated Earth's population, even if that different world might be in the best interest of the global masses that must live and die on an Earth burning more and more each day. I can't blame them for harboring this fear of change. The world at large has not only primed us to fear change and the unknown, but, far too frequently, as history has reminded us time and time again, that we must meet change and the unknown with violence—death the ultimate nullifier of change's promise.

I draft an email to Muñoz. It asks how he's doing, rambles, asks questions about his time in New York. What else to say? What more can be said? Standard email formalities won't cut it. I name-drop a couple colleagues of his whom I know well, hoping to strike up a more substantive conversation. *We have mutuals in common, let's talk.* I want to get out of the impersonal. The impersonal hurts. *What do you like to eat for breakfast? Who was your first love? Why did you want to go grad school, become a theorist?* I have to stop myself. This is an email, not a blind date. Keep it professional.

I don't hit send. I can't bear the idea of my message being just another email from another fan. Can't stand the notion that I am but one among many in my frustratingly bizarre ruminations over a man I have never met. I don't want to imagine my email going unopened and unread.

The theorist of performance performs a grin. There's no doubt about it—he's putting on a show for us. The university office in which he sits becomes a stage that the photographer wants to capture. His boyish smirk, the concentration in his eyes, his hands tip-tapping away at the keyboard in front of him, "working." *José, look... busy, pretend you are working*, the photographer must have said as he snapped the side profile of the theorist. *Look natural.* But are we ever natural when working? The photo is later published in a special 2014 in-memory section of *TDR: The Drama Review*. The caption reads: "José Esteban Muñoz at work in his office at the Department of Performance Studies at New York University." The words emanate a professional seriousness that the grinning, performing Muñoz undercuts.

His colleague, Barbara Browning, as well as many of the performance artists he worked with, contributed the short pieces accompanying this photo, elegies that express their grief and love. The caption indicates that the photo was taken on November 20, 2013, just a few days before December 3, 2013, the date of his death. This must have been one of the last photos taken of him. There was also a last email, a last document saved, a last day working in the office. There must have been some occasion for the taking of this performative photo—a request from a university newsletter, a deadline for a new faculty profile picture. Leading to Muñoz typing away at his desk, studiously productive, staging a performance of the performance studies theorist working in his office. Fitting.

Emails stress me out. Sending them, receiving them. Emails have, for many of us, become our jobs. My job *feels* like it is email. I religiously refresh my email app on my phone because, otherwise, my anxiety over emails accumulating, emails going unattended, stresses me to madness. The genre we call the email is inherently always a request. The email to the literary agent regarding a new manuscript to be looked over. The doctor's office sending over the bill. The university administrator reaching out to find a leader for another new task force. The spammer trying to get sensitive personal information. Requests litter my inbox.

In the twenty-first century, emails are also the bearers of bad news. This is where the rejection letter now lands, where it finds its swiftest means of deliverance. The college rejection, the health insurance claim rejection, the fellowship rejection, the job rejection. The modern century seems mired in rejection. Rejection emails are probably why I have such an aversion to emails in general. I, a writer and academic, know this category of communication all too well. The life of the mind requires the support of others, demands that others believe in you in order for you to make it. While in grad school, I once reached out to a senior scholar asking if they would be willing to be a member of my dissertation committee. Within a few hours they replied with a polite decline—they had no interest in the subject I was writing on. Another scholar entertained the idea of supporting my dissertation research—we even met in person after several email exchanges—only to end with her ghosting me after I sent a follow-up email. I have never heard from her since.

Fellowship and job rejections feel the worst, curt formalities without explanation as to why they rejected you, merely informing you the applicant pool was large and the talent impressive. Before the rejection came you had been imagining all that your life could be with that better-paying job, with that fellowship that would give you time to write. The rejection in the inbox sends you down a spiral of suppressed emotions and histories. Hopelessness kicks in. You've been here before, this is nothing new, yet each time the suffering feels excruciating. What will you do? You complain to partners and friends, take depressive naps or go out for a cocktail or two, continue on because you have to.

For someone who has chosen a career premised upon intellectual or creative production, the rejection email, then, constitutes the most frequent and most banal of inbox events. It is loathed, yet known so well. The language of the rejection email is seen more than the language of an acceptance: "Thank you for your interest in X, but I regret to inform you..."; "X organization received over a thousand applications and can only fund..."; "Though your work is innovative and beautiful, I will unfortunately have to pass on..."

The stakes are low if I send my email to Muñoz. I have nothing to gain, nothing to lose. No one will ever respond. Email loses its power over us when we send it to the dead. We can say whatever we want to say with no consequences. Total epistolary freedom. The inbox the email's grave.

Whenever I walk to the queer bars in the West Village (places I, a happy-hour connoisseur, frequent often), I pass by the building where Muñoz's office was located. It's an unimpressive structure, right on Broadway. The purple NYU Tisch flag waves out front. I stare up at the sixth floor, not knowing which exact window would have been his. The window in the photo of him working in his office could be any of these. Each a windowpane a portal to the sliver of an office inside. I search for an outline akin to Muñoz's in the office photo: a bigger body, slightly hunched over, in a sweater and glasses. I look for the ghost of him in his former office. Hoping for one of the signs from the dead that my Puerto Rican grandmother believed in so passionately—the departed manifesting in a place they had frequented in life, reaching out, communicating, imparting a message. I stand on the bustling sidewalk, staring into the offices above, fantasizing the outline of the theorist at work, a glimpse of him tap-tapping at his desktop computer, concentrated, laser focused on his next book or article, finessing a new concept, developing upon an old idea, toiling away on his next project, which we will never read and never know.

My reverie is cut short by practicality: Why would anyone want to haunt, reside in perpetuity, in their former place of employment?

I can't recall the last photo taken of my brother. He died in 2004, a mere twenty-two years old, before the advent of camera phones. If one wanted to take a photo back in the early aughts, you had to commit to it, go out of your way to lug around a camera and capture a moment of life. In some of the last photos of my brother that I know of, he looks jovial, all big grins and happiness. He was always very outgoing and happy-go-lucky on the surface, but deep down he suffered. He had a depression and a longing for more that I would only come to know about after his death. We found his private writings in one of his dresser drawers, a binder of loose-leaf paper. A treasure discovered from the plundering that happens after a death, when the living swoop in, vulture-like, in hopes of scavenging something that can stand in for the person, a crappy substitute. In an almost illegible scrawl he wrote about our mother, how he hated her. He wrote about his father, whom he had never known, whom he wished he'd known. He wrote about his dreams of leaving New Jersey for another life in someplace like Florida. He wrote rap songs that, to my knowledge, none of my family ever heard him rehearse. The lyrics aren't that good. The lines hit you like an anvil: blunt and forceful and unsatisfying. They sadden me, these lines composed by my brother, because they manifest his uniquely felt pain, his loneliness, his insatiable rage. To anyone who didn't know him—and, as time goes on, as he recedes further into the past, those who steward his memory are fewer and fewer—they are just bad poetry, severed from the context of his life. I'm sure he would have improved his craft had he more time, become like the next Big Pun or Fat Joe, two of his idols. He might have someday become a good lyricist, but that is not the outcome of his story. He wrote, in secret, that he wanted to die. And one day not long after, against his will, not on his own terms, he did.

Photos can never tell the story of an inner life. They merely dance on the surface of things, a surface we can only probe, speculate upon. The beholder projects their desires and fascinations: what they need the photographed person to be in order to make meaning out of a two-dimensional plane. Photos are the performance the photographed want us to see. The performance is the agency they get to hold over their image, their interiority, even after the shot is taken, even after they leave us. The performance in the photo, their means of evading our efforts at constraining them symbolically, metaphorically, for ourselves. Selfish, possessive creatures are the living. The photographed know this, which is why they do what they do, this surface dance we can only, futilely, pathetically, project onto. Their flat and static resistance our arousal.

I took several classes at New York University as a doctoral student through a consortium program. I sat in classrooms in which Muñoz must have lectured, where he must have lobbed some of those exquisitely signature *uhms* into the air. I visited the faculty offices to meet with professors, discuss paper ideas, all the while taking in the office layouts, imagining how Muñoz had once occupied these cramped spaces, pondering the writing he had done there. I even visited one of the faculty apartments owned by NYU in the West Village for a professor's end-of-semester party, all the while thinking of how Muñoz must have decorated his own such apartment, imagining where he'd slept, if he'd used the terrace frequently. During my various forays into classes or lectures hosted at NYU, or even when I simply pass by their many properties on my way somewhere else, I fantasize about Muñoz. Him in his office working, him in his apartment reading, him strolling down the street to class. The area has an aura I associate with Muñoz. My Muñoz.

There is a genre of literature in which writers go on some journey (often physical, but sometimes psychic) to discover more about another writer who means a lot to them. Alice Walker traveling to Florida to write on Zora Neale Hurston. Geoff Dyer traveling to Italy and Mexico to write on D. H. Lawrence. Jenn Shapland in the archives of Carson McCullers. They go seeking some new truth about the writer. They go in pursuit of whom they need the writer to be. The experience transforms them. They tell a story of their own lives through the story of another, an other they never got to know. They visit places that let them glimpse who their beloved writer had been, that let them walk where they had walked. They become a part of an admired writer's story by situating themselves in a certain place.

Where do I go for Muñoz? How do I discover a new truth of him? Perhaps I could begin in Cuba, though he was only there for the first few months of his life, before his family moved to Florida. Hialeah, maybe, where he spent his childhood. Or Duke University, where he spent years working on his doctorate with Eve Sedgwick. But I hedge around the obvious point because I know that his place is New York. He lived here for nearly two decades. Worked at NYU, resided in their housing, wrote about New York City–based performers and artists. The West Village, where NYU is headquartered, I particularly associate with Muñoz. But I find it hard to romanticize (as is often done when writing about one's fixation) the site of NYU. There is no gravestone to visit, no plaque designating the apartment in which he lived. The university is just, well, that—a university. Part and parcel of the gentrified city, buildings encompassing all of Washington Square Park. They would never landmark his former office, nor his university apartment (the waitlist for such housing, I hear, is one many will never get off of), the spaces too lucrative for such memorializing functions. No Muñozian pilgrimage is worth the effort.

The poetics of an email: the salutation of the recipient (if a doctor, make sure to address them as such), the greeting and the *how are you*, the body paragraphs explaining the reason for communication (often a request, a time-sensitive need), the final sentences outlining available times to meet or ways of reaching out, the concluding valediction. The conventions of email not the most exciting genre of writing. Balancing the boundaries of formality and informality, directness and suggestion, getting to the point and giving depth.

Perhaps this is what delays me from hitting *send* on my message to Muñoz. Too many mechanics involved. I don't know how to send an email severed from work, from the transactional, from the demands of the request. I don't know how to make email something else besides what it's become. *Hey, how you are? I miss you. Was thinking of you when I recently read…*

My email to Muñoz, though, also contains the challenge of us being perpetual strangers to one another. Never getting past the first email sent, the banality of greetings and farewells. *Dear Professor Muñoz, How are you doing? My name is Marcos Gonsalez, and we do not know each other. I am reaching out in hopes…*

How crushing, such lines.

I was thirty years old when I got my own office for the first time. Before then, privacy had been at a minimum; spaces in which to work and think in were difficult to attain. In high school, my bedroom wasn't large enough to even hold a desk, so I did my homework and reading on my bed or at the kitchen table. As an undergrad I was fortunate enough to have a desk in my series of cramped dorm rooms, but the hubbub of roommates and college life made the space unideal for writing and thinking. Grad school was the first time in my adult life when my housing had a private bedroom where I could work on my own terms. Because grad school centered on independent studying and writing, I could often work from home rather than go to campus. I quickly realized, however, that working, resting, and sleeping all in the same space wasn't such a good idea. My body could not distinguish between the time meant for work, the time for unwinding, and the time for sleep. The onset of the coronavirus pandemic in 2020 only exacerbated this feeling, since I could no longer go to the library or a café to work.

It wasn't until after grad school, when I began receiving a salary from my first tenure-track job, that I was able to afford an apartment with an extra room for an office. I have never thought so clearly as when I've been inside my *own* office. A room solely dedicated to reading, working, and thinking, where no one can disrupt my concentration by shuffling in or out. I've filled my office with ceiling-height bookcases, with a filing cabinet storing all kinds of documents (museum tickets, playbills, syllabi, exhibition handouts, unpaid bills, unsent postcards), with art. My office is a room of intellective possibility. The first place I have been able to get fully lost in thought, where thought and inquiry are nurtured, where I can play around with ideas. Maintaining this office—and by maintain, I mean continuing to earn enough in order to afford the space—is the difficult part. Twenty-first-century capitalism has commodified every last inch of space, particularly those in cities, making it impossible for anyone not making six figures, or those who don't have a multiple-income household, to secure decent living arrangements. Studio apartments pop up all across cities like New York, an effort to address the lower-income, child-free bracket of earners, the rents exorbitantly high for a live-in box. Indeed, these rents are unaffordable for those of average income, like me, who don't even qualify for these awfully small quarters that have income requirements.

Even though there are plenty of opportunities and spaces to house everyone, we must continue to get robbed by greedy landlords lining their pockets off overpriced units, to see low-income folks settle for hellish studios or their parents' basements, to see the most vulnerable go unhoused altogether because capitalism demands that our housing cater above all to the wealthy. "Having a home office is a privilege," I once heard a university administrator say, an attempt to cajole disgruntled faculty demanding higher wages to meet the cost of living in the city in which they worked. Sure, let's call it a privilege, but the privilege framework ultimately just muddles the core problem: cost of living keeps going up, and employers don't want to pay up. The bourgeoisie bosses want the common worker to work hard and work a lot, to dedicate our lives to the altar of capitalist profit, with no tangible benefits to ourselves. Not even the bare minimum guarantee of wages that will get us a proper house to live in! Why work so hard under these conditions? Disaffection and resentment have become the logical end results of such stubborn capitalist greed.

We all deserve to have a space to think in, even those of us who aren't writers, artists, or academics. A designated room in which to reflect and contemplate, apart from the routines of the kitchen, the sanctum of the bedroom, the noise and activity of the living room. A room to be alone in. An office really isn't a luxury, and when we think of it as so—when we agree that having multiple rooms is a privilege that only some can afford—that's when the bosses and the landlords win. The center can no longer hold. Why not fall through like Alice, curious about the rabbit hole's end, and see what's on the other side?

Bloch, pulling a sentence from the German philosopher and playwright Friedrich Schiller—"That which never happened anywhere, that alone never gets old"—remixes the phrase to serve his own utopian philosophy: "That which has *never entirely* happened *anywhere,* but which is *to come as a human event and which defines the task*, that will never grow old."[13]

We not only need an office in order to think better, we also need to be able to leave it. Muñoz, while discussing the performer Fred Herko in *Cruising Utopia*, includes a detail about having written this section of the book in proximity to the apartment in which Herko died by suicide. Muñoz intentionally walks over to the West Village apartment: "As I neared finishing writing this chapter, I walked to 5 Cornelia Street. This was a morbid little homage, a private performance fueled by minor and abstract necrophilic attachment. This stroll made me think about the abstraction of writing about a suicide 'as performance' and how that misses something. I did not expect to feel much, but my expectations proved wrong."[14] The stroll through the neighborhood, the theorist as flaneur, proves to be an instance of performance, a thinking-performance. He clears his mind while strolling in order to finish the chapter.

Muñoz describes his solitary strolling meditation on suicide as a "private performance." Perhaps he uses this phrase to seem modest in comparison to the purposefully, flamboyantly performative archive of Herko, but perhaps he is also saying more. Performance is usually thought to require an audience in order to make it real. Muñoz's "private performance" seems like an oxymoron. If one performs only for oneself, is it still performance? Muñoz suggests that we can and do, to generative effect. His "private performance" shows us what goes into the making of new ideas. It is the theorist's own performance on theorizing about performance. It goes on display for us, the readers, a subtle breaking of the fourth wall between text and audience. It is not sequestered in the private realm but is all too public, performed before the passersby on his meditative stroll, before the audience of readers who will continue to read and reread the theorist's strolling. And it addresses the query of performance studies scholar Ramón H. Rivera-Servera—"What does performance *do* to shape or change the social realm?"—by showing that the social world responds even to events that unfold underwhelmingly, unostentatiously, like a stroll one takes to clear the mind.[15]

"That which has *never entirely* happened *anywhere,* but which is *to come as a human event and which defines the task*, that will never grow old."

Cruising Utopia gives us another glimpse into the theorist's childhood, as *Disidentifications* did, the private life of the theorist made public. The theorist is around five years old, relatives have just arrived from Cuba, and the men are watching boxing on the television. Muñoz writes: "I walk across the red-brick floor and momentarily cross the screen. Then my oldest cousin calls out, 'Look at the way he walks, how he shakes his ass. I wish I had a girlfriend who walked like that!' The other men in the room erupt into laughter."[16] He cannot understand precisely what it is they're jeering at, but he feels their mockery. Feels the "amazingly painful" experience of being singled out as queer—though not yet knowing that is the term for it. As Sedgwick expressed in a footnote of her marvelously titled essay, "How to Bring Your Kids Up Gay," such moments "have for many of us been formative childhood experiences of difference and stigmatization";[17] the event of others recognizing one's queerness, the unfolding of an identity in a swish of the hips.

Like Muñoz, I had others flag my queerness as a kid. The hip-swish my mother would see to correct. The too-limp wrist that my brother would point out as unfit for a boy. The lisp mocked by classmates. Identified cruelly by others before I could identify myself.

The theorist as a child would convert the mockery and humiliation into a learning moment through the act of contemplation. Thought as an early tool of his resistance: "I wanted to, needed to know: what was it about my body and the way I moved it through the world that was so off, so different? I studied movement from then on, watching the way in which women walked and the way in which men walked."[18] He studied in order to ape the proper gestures of masculinity and heterosexuality, to pass in a world horrifyingly violent toward those who defy gender conformity. But the mimicry is never wholly convincing. Another "fey boy" spotted the ruse, Muñoz writes, and "took me aside in junior high and told me that I pulled my books too close to my chest like a girl."[19]

I too tried to butch up as a teenager. Pass myself off as a respectably masculine queer. Discipline myself into gendered conformity, let others discipline me. I failed. Splendidly failed. The wrists too limp and the hips too swishy and the mouth too lisping to suppress.

......

Muñoz writes of the other "fey boy": "Part of me wants to encounter him again, now in a gay space, a march, a club, a bathhouse, and embrace him like a fellow survivor, somebody else who made it through. Yet I imagine him at home, in Miami, with a wife who might remind him every once in a while how he should position his legs when he sits down while visiting his in-laws."[20]

Muñoz lived in the New York City of the 1990s and 2000s, which was very different from the one I live in now. He lived in a network of artists and critics running about the city, high off cheap rents, cheap taxis, and cheaper living. He saw experimental theater flourish, saw performance artists of varying races and classes doing the most in the clubs. Later, he witnessed the "cleaning up" of Times Square, a process of gentrification set in motion by Mayor Rudy Giuliani, documented in Samuel R. Delany's 1999 essay collection, *Times Square Red, Times Square Blue* (a text Muñoz wrote about). He was here during 9/11 and its aftermath, as he wrote about in a pedagogy essay. He visited queer clubs in Manhattan and Queens spending time in those spaces so that he could later theorize upon them in his books, noting how one day the clubs were there and the next they were gone. This was the New York City that marks Muñoz's entire body of work, making possible the artists he came in contact with and the analyses he produced.

Muñoz and I shared the same New York for three years—starting with my arrival in 2010, ending with his death in 2013—but that New York was already so different from the one he'd come to know in the 1990s, when he started his job at NYU. The New York that greeted me as a precocious eighteen-year-old was one of unaffordable rents and high prices. Splurging on a drunken night out and a cab ride home would mean a skipped dinner (or two) to make up for the costs of such opulence. I have watched the city expand its army of cops through the years, to harass children jumping the turnstiles and unhoused folks sleeping on subway platforms. At Rikers, the island jail overstuffed with incarcerated humans, conditions have worsened year by year, inmates dying at alarming rates, the carceral state consolidating its power in order to make the wealthy few feel "safe" in the big city. The New York I have lived through is one where artists and critics can no longer afford to build a life as our elders did, those who came before us with no money to their name but still made it, Warhol, Ginsberg, Haring, their names now monetized by the same city officials and the bourgeoisie who are actively erasing the material conditions that gave rise to such innovators in the first place. Under twenty-first-century capitalism, New York artists and intellectuals cannot create communities organized around experimenting with aesthetics, sexuality, ideas, gender expression, or forms of living. At least, not together in person. Perhaps social media and online forums will host the next great wave of the avant-garde. But I am not too sure about that either because no matter where we are in the world, capitalism still stifles, interjects. Even when you're behind a computer screen or your phone, your rent is still too high, your credit card and student debt are through the roof, you're working too much, your attention span is absolutely shot from the stress of it all. Internet prices continue to surge too, further hampering the prospect of your digital avant-garde! Where and when can art and ideas still flourish, under the global conditions we all must endure?

There has never been a utopia in New York. No true utopia can blossom on stolen land whose keepers refuse to return it—who refuse, even, to admit that a violence has taken place, refuse to atone materially or structurally for all the enslaved and exploited who were forced to build a society, brick by brick. The New York of the 1960s, 1970s, or 1980s was by no means even close to utopia, especially for folks of color. But there were glimmers of possibility that we can mine for a politics of the utopic. A utopia we have yet to see, that may require revolutionary gusto, a demolition-like impulse that isn't afraid of a world entirely strange to this one. We may not have Wilde's map, but we can work to draw it.

. . . . . .

D. A. Miller on Barthes on utopia: "Every utopia secretes signs of the conflict that it fulfills the wish to abolish; these signs must be read so long as utopian vision animates, rather than replaces, a labor of bringing it to pass."[21] Admittedly, I'm not entirely sure what Miller means here, but something about it feels profound. Hypothesis: All utopias contain the original conflict they sought to supersede. The social issue, human tyranny, oppression. Somewhere embedded into that perfect society, that as-yet-unachieved society, the conflict lies dormant. One cannot lose sight of this conflict, this origin story—otherwise, one loses the utopic, too. The conflict as a historical context that utopia needs in order to fulfill itself. Utopia isn't all sunshine and roses, I want to think Miller is saying.

Miller's enigmatic prose often stops me in my tracks, as it does here. Regardless, I can't help but feel dazzled by his abstruseness.

Another photo of Muñoz in his office: a brooding, bespectacled, cropped-haired theorist who stares back at the viewer. He wears a navy-blue sweater, his books displayed behind him. He's standing up, unlike the 2002 video primer on performance studies or the 2013 photo of him grinning at his desk. He looks older than in the 2002 video, younger than in the photo of 2013. This has to be the Muñoz of *Cruising Utopia.* The theorist in his prime, about to publish or perhaps having just published his second monograph. The theorist readying himself for the next project, in his brooding midlife phase.

My head contains an album of all these Muñozian images. Photos, stills from the videos, all assembled in some composite of the theorist. I flip through its pages, poke at the bear of a question of who Muñoz truly was, a question that is impossible to answer. Downright futile, for a stranger like me. But I keep on shuffling through images, watch them transmogrify into distortions, half-truths, and half-fictions, the theorist younger and the theorist older, my personal album kept close.

I send my message to the email address on Muñoz's faculty profile page. It reads:

Dear José (if I may)

How are you? I hope your semester is going well. My name is Marcos Gonsalez, and we have never met. We will never meet, unfortunately, unless, that is, we can count this email as our first, official meeting. I was writing for many reasons, all of which I cannot precisely identify. I know my motive is in the right place. I know I need to send this email to you. I mainly mean to reach out because, though it be a faux pas in professional emails such as this one to say what I am about to say, you mean so much to me. To call you an idol is cliché, and inexact. The connotation implies a relation (one many have to celebrities) that is reverential, fan-like, or rudimentarily hagiographic. You are not that for me yet you are, in fact, more than that. Inexpressible, what you are, hence why I write this email. Why I write to you. Email seems an unlikely venue in which to extend such an appreciation, to espouse the sentiment that you have changed my life. But I do so via email because it is all I have. All I have with you is this email I send.

Maybe what I mean to say is that sometimes I sit on one of the benches in Washington Square Park, near to where you lived and worked, imagining that at some point and time, you sat right where I sat, saw what I saw. My here and now, your then and there, on a bench in Manhattan. My favorite time to visit the park is in the Fall or Spring, when it's not too hot or too cold. I watch as university students cluster in groups around the fountain to gossip or horse around. I notice the musicians practicing a new tune, dancers trying out a new movement, actors performing monologues in hopes they nail the audition. Skateboards crash against pavement and a voice booms from a megaphone protesting something, all startling me, stunned the elders nearby do not wake from their midday snooze. The park always has commotion, people doing their many different things, all ages carousing about in a chaotic thrash of life. There is a messy politic that seems to attract those that come to hang in the park. We come here because we know all of us are so different, different ways of passing time and killing boredom, different sensibilities, but all united in the love of the anarchic sprawl. I like to think this is what attracted you to the park, too.

The micro-society of the park is not a utopia, by any means. Cops patrol vigilantly in the neoliberal city, defending the property of the landlords and the investments of the rich, the unhoused and the cruising queers a remnant of the park's past. Rents keep soaring, food prices keep increasing, wages stay stagnant. Your Washington Square Park, your New York City, José, is probably not mine, our views unrecognizable to the other. But there's a kernel of utopic dissent, I think, across space and time, in your Washington Square Park and mine, in everyone who has lounged in this park, who harbored in them at least a single thought, whether they acknowledged it or not, whether they could perceive it or not, that the city—perhaps even the world—could be different. No cops, no poverty, no white supremacy, no billionaires. I believe in this kernel of utopic dissent, suppressed though it may be, across our differences, looking differently to each and every one of us. Holding to the belief that utopia has resided in our minds, at some point in time, we who have convened in this place.

I have gotten ahead of myself, José. Apologies. I can't help but daydream. I come from a long line of people who have dreamed of a different world. Who risked life, and death, in search of this other place. To wax sentimental: I sit on a bench in Washington Square Park, honestly, to think of you. Constructing a timeline where we got to meet, in person, in a class or conference, connecting by our shared identities, our shared goals in forging a more utopic world, culminating, in some future point, in us sitting on a bench in Washington Square Park. Colleagues, friends perhaps. We both liked the chisme. We both liked superhero comics. I fantasize, often, about events that never happened, and will never happen. Sheer speculation, rewritings, alternative histories. I think this practice is important. I think it is life-sustaining and life-nourishing. I believe this because so much of queer life, and queer of color life in particular, has always been brutally defined by curtailed storylines and compromised histories. We know intimately about violated childhoods, and adulthoods equally violated. We know the ravage of disease, the ravage of poverty, the ravage of violence that, if not taking our lives outright, traumatizes them, another form of claiming life without needing us gone. I don't want to bring the mood down, José. But when I think of you I think of us on that park bench. I think of this past that wasn't our past, this future that will never be our future. It is how I spend time with you. Being with you against the odds of the oppressively pragmatic dichotomies that are life and death, past and present, the living and the dead, the worlds we no longer inhabit, together. Realism blows.

Let me conclude this email. I have taken up enough of your time, José. You may not even have gotten to these final lines. You are busy, after all. Please keep up the work. Keep on transforming lives, as you have done mine.

Yours,

Marcos Gonsalez

IV

SUIT JACKET INFORMALITIES

1

He's in a black suit jacket and a brown collared shirt that's buttoned all the way up to the neck—not the version of the theorist I am used to. In no other photo or video have I seen him so stiffly professional like this one, uploaded to YouTube. I know him in a turtleneck, or in a button-up loosened around the collar. But he dons this garb for his mentor and friend Eve Sedgwick, who has won the 1998 Kessler Award, whom he is introducing before she gives her Kessler Lecture. Given annually by CLAGS: The Center for LGBTQ Studies, the award honors a scholar who has made a significant impact in the field. After Muñoz's introduction, Sedgwick will read from her then-forthcoming book, *A Dialogue on Love*, which recounts her time in therapy through memoir, poetry, and even her therapist's notes. The highly innovative hybrid work will be published in 1999, the same year as Muñoz's *Disidentifications*.

Muñoz's ten-minute speech betrays the professionalism the suit jacket is supposed to convey: his words are not formal but rather jocular and loving, full of both lighthearted jokes and doting admiration for his former teacher. "If I thought about Eve," he begins, "I knew she would like it if I roasted her a little, teased her in my ever so loving way. I could always talk about how Eve's mind is one of the most powerful and twisted engines in all of creation. How it reads, how it shows the errors of some of the ways we were taught to read B.E.—before Eve." He queries his old Duke classmates in attendance who had also worked with Eve, asking them to share their thoughts on her character. Gus Stadler: "[Eve] taught me how to honor shyness . . . to see it as a source of fucking power." Jennifer Doyle: "Don't fuck with Eve." Their use of "fuck" prompts Muñoz to quip, "What are they telling us? What about Eve inspires students to talk dirty?" Laughter roars from the crowd. He's funny, devilishly charming, unlike the image of seriousness I have crafted in my head. Is it the suit? This brilliantly witty version of the theorist is, like the suit jacket, new to me.

It must be his teacher, his friend, who brings it out in him. In his writings and his other public appearances, the theorist is much more somber. It is a difficult task to make theory humorous, after all. Theory's currency is seriousness. Theory must take itself seriously. For legitimacy, for relevancy, for any hope of being taken seriously to effect change. Theory strives to sway minds, change them, and change is no laughing matter. Very few can find the humor in theory appropriately, let alone effectively. (Derrida an exception.) The window for misfires in such an undertaking is huge, leaving lots of room to rub the wrong way or downright offend. Sedgwick was one of the rare thinkers who could pull it off. After all, she was a theorist of pleasure, and her work was driven by that pleasure. She was one of the first to show that theory can be a pleasurable undertaking for both theorist and reader. Consider, for instance, the pleasurably eye-catching title of her 1989 Modern Language Association paper: "Jane Austen and the Masturbating Girl." The paper scandalized conference goers at the time who would rather not have thought of sex—or, more to the point, of Austen and sex, or, to put an even finer point on it, of Austen and masturbation—as a site of scholarly inquiry. She later developed the paper into an essay that would further scandalize literary critics upon publication in *Critical Inquiry* in 1991, and then again, in 1993, as part of *Tendencies*. "Bedroom scenes are not so commonplace in Jane Austen's novels that readers get jaded with the chiaroscuro of sleep and passion, wan light, damp linen, physical abandon, naked dependence, and the imperfectly clothed body," she muses, as if trolling her haters, as if flaunting how very, *very* closely between the lines she will be reading in order to evidence her thesis of female autoeroticism across Austen's oeuvre.[1] Sedgwick's interpretive promiscuities shocked her detractors not so much because of her explicit take on that darling of the British literary canon, but more because she was able to graph any narrative or descriptive detail onto the thesis she was proposing. And with such singular style, too. Concerning *Sense and Sensibility*'s Marianne Dashwood: "[Autoeroticism] signifies an excess of sexuality altogether, an excess dangerous to others but chiefly to herself: the chastening illness that ultimately wastes her physical substance is both the image and the punishment of the 'distracted' sexuality that, continually 'forgetting itself,' threatens, in her person, to subvert the novel's boundaries between the public and the private."

Put bluntly: Her haters were outright jealous. They couldn't help but take a peek at what she'd cooked up because they wished they'd been able to do the same. They couldn't stand that she was having such a good time doing theory. The joke was always on them.

Sedgwick taught where I went to graduate school, though our paths, like Muñoz's and mine, never crossed. By the time I arrived in 2014, she had already passed away, in 2009. Professors continued to talk about her reverentially, lovingly, though none of the students in my cohort ever knew her. But she was a queer theory lodestar and we all knew it, all felt some connection to her singular style because our professors kept her memory alive in the classrooms and hallways. We knew Eve Sedgwick as an absent presence. A ghost whose haunting we didn't mind.

......

"I want to speculate that as much as [*Between Men*] did to advance the progress of what became known, for a moment, as queer theory," wrote Wayne Koestenbaum of Sedgwick, his friend and colleague, in his foreword to the thirtieth-anniversary edition of her now-classic *Between Men*. "It also encouraged—within critical work undertaken by scholars roused to emulation—the poetic freedom to choose at *pleasure*, with the understanding that pleasure is never a simple matter, never a rudimentary case or hydraulic release or frothy *jouissance*."[2] I believe Koestenbaum is saying of his friend that her research was guided by the pleasure of choice. She chose to study the texts that gave her pleasure, chose to put the unlikeliest texts together for the unlikeliest readings. Choice, for Sedgwick, seems to become a matter of pleasure in and of itself.

Why would a queer theorist haunt the halls of their former place of employment?—a question I frequently return to. I can't help but fix the thinker in the halls of the university. Maybe it's because I don't know where else to look. The college a graveyard for visiting the dead.

I have only worn a suit jacket a handful of times in my life, exclusively for weddings and job interviews. The attire is too butch and formal for my limp-wristed homosexual sensibilities. I put the jacket on and I feel boxy, square, my pronounced shoulders more pronounced. On several occasions I have seriously contemplated getting my shoulders shaved down, an expensive and apparently excruciating procedure, undertaken by the likes of (allegedly) Michael Jackson.

"The keyword for me is pleasure," Muñoz says at the Kessler Lecture. "Eve has helped me never lose track of pleasure. Its place and its role and how things get really boring when we don't track, own, deploy, relish, and even honor pleasure." Sedgwick's emphasis on pleasure is rare among theorists. Maybe this is why so many readers find theory boring. They can't find the theorist's pleasure in their own theorizing. They don't know why they themselves should feel pleasure from reading it.

True, not all theory calls for pleasure in the way that Sedgwick's or Muñoz's work does. Certain topics do not demand displays of pleasure in thought. Certain topics do not evoke—or need to evoke, for that matter—pleasure in the audience. If pleasure is involved in theory, it must commingle with deep reflection, strategic action, and radical transformation. Pleasure is like a sauce to theory: making it savory or, like a spice, adding kick. Moreover, theory does not always produce the immediate effect of pleasure. In fact, odds are that the opposite occurs. Theory can be jarring to read since most theory challenges preexisting logics and systems. Some ideas discomfit, some are hard to process, some disturb to the core. I have experienced this intimately, especially in my early days of reading Muñoz. The lessons were *too* real, too close to home.

However, in the end, I hold firmly to the belief that the transformation that theory sparks—the new knowing and new sense of what the world can be—results in pleasure. The pleasure of knowing a little better your place in the world and what that means. The pleasure of knowing not all is what it seems, even though we are told repeatedly that it *is* what it seems, no questions or concerns required. The pleasure of knowing that more can be done. I want to believe that a changed relation to self and world can induce pleasure. The theorist's speech at the Kessler Lecture performs the lessons he learned from his mentor: The pleasure of thought. How thinking can be shot through with the comedic. How theory can be far from dull.

Sedgwick mentions Muñoz in the acknowledgments of her 1993 essay collection, *Tendencies*. He was still her graduate student at the time. She identifies him as a thinker of original queer thought, predicting, like the academic Oracle of Delphi, his genius to come. In her opening remarks to her Kessler Lecture, she names him as one of her "big heroes."

......

"Most importantly, she's taught me how the best thinking is intractably attached to pleasure. Queer thinking is a thinking that never loses sight of pleasure."

Muñoz makes another appearance in the acknowledgements of his mentor's 2003 essay collection, *Touching Feeling*. This time he is officially no longer her student but a full-fledged professor—a theorist, like her.

In his essay collection *My 1980s & Other Essays*, Wayne Koestenbaum recounts attending Sedgwick's "electrifying" talk at the 1989 MLA conference, "How to Bring Your Kids Up Gay: The War on Effeminate Boys." He recalls, "I'll never forget the moment when she described the 'effeminate boy' as 'the haunting abject of gay thought itself': as if in *Last Year at Marienbad*'s many-mirrored hall, I hallucinated serried ranks of junior nellies, awaiting description and embrace."

Sedgwick opened her talk with her crisply stated, "It's always open season on gay kids."[3] She ended by critiquing the mainstream psychiatric and psychoanalytic view of queer boys: "The wish for the dignified treatment of already-gay people is necessarily destined to turn into either trivializing apologetics or, much worse, a silkily camouflaged complicity in oppression—in the absence of a strong, explicit, *erotically invested* affirmation of some people's felt desire or need that there be gay people in the immediate world."[4] Sedgwick turns conference stodginess on its head, her ornate syntax defying standard academic prose. "Munificently, Eve transformed sissy shame from unfortunate idiosyncrasy into golden exemplarity—to be resumed, annotated, politicized, and enshrined in art."[5]

The pleasure of theory, the sexiness of thought—Muñoz in his suit jacket, Sedgwick at the MLA conference.

......

Many know of my Muñoz fascination. Of what the theorist means to me. The scholar and author Rachel Corbman, while researching in the Sedgwick archive at Duke University, sends me an image of a postcard that Muñoz once mailed to Sedgwick and some of his other Duke professors. The postcard is dated July 30, 1991. The postmark identifies the sender's location as Florida. It was summer break, and the theorist must have been visiting his parents in Hialeah. The front of the postcard appears to be crafted via homemade collage work. It shows two people in dresses who look to be pasted into a tropical setting. The one in the green dress looks to be a man in a wig, presumably in drag. Behind him is an alligator, its mouth open, trying to chomp down on his butt. Behind the alligator is the second person, wearing a pink dress, holding open the alligator's mouth. Muñoz has superimposed a cutout of his face onto the person in pink's. His face has been jaggedly ripped from another photograph and is held down by tape. He can't be any older than twenty-three in the cutout, the most youthful image of the theorist I have yet seen, his chin like Jay Leno's, his head topped with a San Francisco Giants baseball cap. His message is written on the other side of the postcard.

"*Queridos*," he says, "Here you see me goofing around with one of my gal pals by the pool." He mentions seeing *Boyz n the Hood* and getting a few ideas from the film. (I have yet to track down any mentions of the film in his work or pinpoint how exactly those ideas may have made their way into one of his theories.) He references the recent arrest of Paul Reubens, who'd been masturbating in a theater—"I can't believe they finally got Pee-Wee! I'm only a couple of hours away, so if worst comes to worst I'll bust him out." Muñoz, the goofball. He writes that he feels rested and looks forward to returning to Durham for his studies.

"The jokes that mean the most to you are the ones you don't quite get," theorized Sedgwick in an essay that Muñoz included in his 1996 coedited anthology on Andy Warhol, *Pop Out*.[6]

......

Muñoz, in his Kessler Lecture speech, describes Sedgwick's comportment: A "woman with a very small cracking voice and a blushing presence manages to completely fill up a room in ways that really throw off the usual suspects. Voices that seem to never crack and feel all too comfortable with themselves."

Theory and humor are strange bedfellows, but friendship draws them into closer orbit. Friendship makes theory a bit wacky and strange. Fodder for the haters.

Lauren Berlant, in a preface to a 2019 anthology of writings on Sedgwick, meditates upon "the perceptual universe of Eve's work." They ask, "How do we continue the project of coming to terms with what we can't specifically have asked for, the shocking impact of the radical reframing, stylistic challenge, theoretical elaboration, historical materialism, mode of focus and attention, and genre lability that mark what it meant, and still means, to be writing with Eve not just on, but in, our minds?"[7] Berlant, like Sedgwick, passed away from cancer, in 2021.

1998 feels like a lifetime ago. The seven-year-old child that was me that year is a distant memory, a stranger. Everything feels so long ago when it is now.

From Jacques Derrida's *The Post Card*: "I would like to write you so simply, so simply, so simply. Without having anything ever catch the eye, excepting yours alone, and what is more while erasing all the traits, even the most inapparent ones, the ones that mark the tone, or the belonging to a genre (the letter for example, or the post card), so that above all the language remains self-evidently secret, as if it were being invented at every step, and as if it were burning immediately, as soon as any third party would set eyes on it (speaking of which, when will you agree that we effectively burn all this ourselves?)."[8]

2

There's no suit jacket in sight. He wears but a tan collared shirt, several of the buttons undone at the top, the sleeves ever so slightly rolled up, arm hair exposed. A plain white T-shirt beneath. In this 2003 lecture he is informality itself. The hour-long video takes place in a lecture hall at Hamilton College. He speaks on queerness and Latinidad, an early foray into the topics that will dominate his last, posthumous book, *The Sense of Brown*. He discourses on Latin American celebrities like Shakira and Ricky Martin and queer representation on mainstream television shows like *Queer Eye for the Straight Guy*. He peppers jokes throughout, his humor at work. There's a lectern before him, which he frequently grasps on both sides. When he does this grasping he hunches over, elbows at ninety-degree angles, flexing and unflexing, his body shimmying about. I don't know if he is nervous. I don't think he is. This is something more like the body in thought. The theorist's body performing thought. The performance of thinking through awkwardly positioned elbows.

In each video, each presentation, he is so different. Young Muñoz bearing no similarity to the older, more restrained Muñoz that I see in recordings from the early 2010s. I don't know this 2003 Muñoz either.

But I do pick up on his goofiness, which is looking more and more like a signature of his with every video I watch. The theorist with a sense of humor. The theorist who can let his hair down and be silly. The theorist becoming one's friend.

In 1996, Eve Sedgwick edited a collection of poems, stories, and diary entries written by her late student and friend Gary Fisher. The two met when Sedgwick was a visiting professor at the University of California, Berkeley; Fisher was enrolled in her gay and lesbian literature course. Fisher died in 1994 from AIDS-related complications, a writer still unpublished. Sedgwick undertook the task of publishing his work posthumously with Duke University Press, titling the result *Gary in Your Pocket*. Before his death, Fisher and Sedgwick had decided on the title and cover image together. The book collects his diary entries, which begin in 1977 and record his thoughts on his upbringing, literature, interracial dating, sex, and death, among other topics. From 1987 onwards, there are also letters addressed to Sedgwick. There are more notebooks and journals in Fisher's archive, housed at the James C. Hormel LGBTQIA Center, San Francisco Public Library, which, according to scholar Ellis Hanson, contain "many variations on the phrase 'I LOVE YOU, EVE.'"[9]

The book garnered mixed reactions, particularly because Fisher, who was Black, described in his diary entries scenes of sexual humiliation and gratifying debasement at the hands of white men. In some, Fisher is called the N-word and fantasizes about slave/master dynamics. "So I'm on my knees again, before God," reads the journal entry of March 29, 1987. "Tall, white, wary of me, trying to work him into a froth of masterliness. Sucking a man's cock makes him bolder meaner, or one hopes, and even if it wasn't so in this Superman's case, his big hands, touching me anywhere were part threat." The narrator, "wanting to optimize his self-pleasure even and knowing that he was desiring that I should swallow his manseed, feeling that in him, the desire to feed me, nurse me as he feeds himself on my nursing him, feeds his ego, his manness, his very strength, I hope."[10] On November 9, 1984, he reports on an orgy he'd attended with his white lover, Roy: "How much cock did I taste at my orgy in Hinton James? two? three? all of them? who came in my ass? How many bathroom boys down my eager throat? How much poison seed? How much of my death wish had I realized then? Funny, I have no reason to ask why here because I know. I only have one big regret—that I won't suck a million more, that I won't suck that special one (whoever it belongs to) a million times; that I won't be folded up and made one with a stud."[11] The fact that Sedgwick, a white woman, had edited and was championing this work made for an even more uneasy reception to the text, then and now.

In 2013, which would be the year of his passing, Muñoz published the essay "Race, Sex, and the Incommensurate," extensively analyzing

Gary in Your Pocket, Sedgwick's editorial role in it, and the incommensurability at the heart of this collaboration between a white woman and gay Black man. He presents this essay as a continuation of the thinking he had started in *Cruising Utopia*, on the relation to queerness and politics. This time, though, he wants to meditate upon "queerness as a sense of the incalculable and, simultaneously, the incalculable sense of queerness."[12] He understands Fisher's sexuality and relationship to Sedgwick as an "experience of being-in-common-in-difference," a connection activated not through equivalences, or shared identities, but a shared ethos of difference. The incommensurabilities between Fisher's writing and Sedgwick's editorship, between their very different identities and lives, do not align with the normative logics of neoliberal recognition and valuation. Why, for instance, was a white heterosexual woman so interested in promoting the work of a Black gay writer who detailed his fantasies of being a slave to white men? Why could she not have found a Black editor to contextualize and present the volume? These uncomfortable questions about white editorship over Black posthumous authorship, writes Muñoz, are precisely what unlock another kind of commons, another kind of politic that does not seek respectability, neat narratives, or homogeneity when expressing queer of color subjectivity. He admits that it took him years to wrap his head around Fisher's work and Sedgwick's interest in it. His mentor's commitment to Fisher's work went beyond friendship, he speculates, and had more to do with the "sharing (out) of the unshareable that she too participates in."[13] Riffing off Jean-Luc Nancy, Muñoz uses "the sharing of the unshareable" to summarize Fisher's sexually charged and stylistically daring work: the acts and desires Fisher shares with the reader even though modesty and decorum would tell him not to, and Sedgwick's editorial oversight of it—she too sharing with audiences what respectability would otherwise tell her to keep private.

Writer and editor, student and the teacher, Black and white, man and woman, living and dead—an incommensurable setup, a relation of overexposure, an oversharing sensibility. The formalities upholding these dynamics tensing toward another configuration. The informal excites.

I read *Gary in Your Pocket* in graduate school. It was required reading for one of my classes on African American literature. Though the class was taught by a Black professor, the room was loaded with predominately white students. The discomfort Muñoz described as surrounding the book was exactly the atmosphere in the class the day it was discussed. No one, myself included, knew what to do with this book that shocked, that overshared, that didn't care for decorum. The air was thick with unease.

My contribution to the discussion that day was something about Fisher's style, especially in the diaries. Like Sedgwick in her afterword, I expressed awe for how he had composed words, for the abrasive honesty of his desires. I felt unnerved, too. "You soothe that child in me, Roy, every time you put your cock in me or your balls on me," he writes, addressing his lover on March 26, 1984. "I love looking up into the hairy, square dominance of it all—your face with that bit of question in it, your wracked body and the proffered nipples still red from attention. If you knew what you were doing to me there would be no question—you couldn't get deep enough, I don't think, if you did that child would curl up beneath you in a massive soul-releasing sigh—every time, all the time—no one can get that deep."[14] On one level, Fisher is describing an instance of routine sadomasochism, but it is also more than that. The writing also pulls the reader into the scene. We are given perspective—what it's like to look up at the hairy chest and the erect nipples of a man—and we are given the looker's introspection, what he feels as he stares up at what he desires so feverishly. Fisher longs for a deepness that is, according to him, impossible to give. He wants it deep, deep, and deeper, a deepness of self-annihilation, but "every time, all the time" he fails to reach this goal. The failing is inevitable but he gets on his knees anyway, hoping nonetheless as the man towers above him, erect.

In class that day my analysis seemed to snowball all over the place as I attempted to summarize, to make sense of, the unsummarizable. Other students stumbled too. All we did was stumble over interpretation. Interpretation's insufficiencies.

"every time, all the time"—this refrain of failure, the always that is "every time" and the forever that is "all the time." Stuck knowing that no matter how many times one tries to reach the point of satisfaction—fulfillment? climax? destruction?—it is unachievable. Too deep to reach.

Maybe it wasn't necessarily Fisher that was hard to talk about that day in class. Maybe it was the fact we were trying to talk about sex—what it means, how it undoes us—but were not quite exactly sure how to do so. How to account for when the literary can be erotic. How the particulars of another's sex life can be scrutinized by the lexicons and tools of literary criticism. I'm sure none of us had taken a class dedicated to analyzing literary depictions of sex. It would be a great class, don't get me wrong, but not one routinely on the curriculum in college literature programs. Bringing up sex in any context of our society is still taboo.

There is a notable difference between reading about sex in literature and critically analyzing what you've read. Simply reading about sex can be done privately. Analysis requires you to actually talk about sex, to make sex available for interpretation and discussion. Analyzing sex requires another to hear your aesthetic judgment on how that sex functions in the text, how it is represented, and what else it might mean besides just sex. Sex leaps out from the privacy of the domestic when we analyze it. Out of the closet of shame we readily confine it to.

There is no indication that Muñoz and Fisher ever crossed paths. Muñoz makes no mention of it in his essay. They attended graduate programs on opposite sides of the country, writing in styles vastly different from one another. Fisher shared abundantly about his life, while Muñoz curated carefully what the reader would and wouldn't know about him. Fisher enjoyed the freedoms of the creative writer, while Muñoz maintained the critical distance of the scholar.

Their only commonality: Sedgwick. The mentor who cared deeply for them both. The students who cared deeply for the mentor. A thread of unexpected intimacy.

"every time, all the time"—my attempts, my failings, at figuring out what Muñoz means to me. Who Muñoz is *for* me and *to* you.

Sedgwick refers to Fisher frequently throughout her therapy book, *A Dialogue on Love*. She visits him in California, worrying over his health. She discusses him in sessions, talks of how much he means to her. She describes the process of collecting his writings. "A few hours with some of Gary's papers, which I'll be editing for publication: two-hundred-proof taste of what the coming months hold as I plunge into the vat of his unmakings. Including, intensely: abyssal, glazed-over boredom." She continues: "This kind of boredom doesn't mean no-cathexis: this kind, to me, means overstimulation, stimulation of wrong or dangerous kinds; hell; rape; dissolution. The kind of boring that's a penetration."[15]

The work of publishing the book of a student and friend, after their death, when they can no longer give input for their vision, demands considerable care, attention, and grace. It is an intense practice of devotion. Muñoz's friend, Tavia Nyong'o, and his former student, Joshua Chambers-Letson, edited the theorist's unfinished third monograph *The Sense of Brown*, for publication. Student editing teacher, teacher editing student, friend editing friend. These editorial labors of love.

Sedgwick's 1994 poetry collection, *Fat Art, Thin Art*, contains "A Vigil," a poem about Fisher. "Gary, have you ever heard of a deity, / maybe a Hindu one, who's an elephant?"[16] the poem asks. It shows us

Gary lying in a hospital bed, a bottle-green oxygen mask latched to his face, a tube snaking out. You look like Ganesh, she tells him. The teacher holds his hand, sits by his side. His disease will take him, will require Sedgwick to compile his only work for publication. At times during the poem he seems to swat her away, and she is unable to determine the intent behind his motions—if he is fatigued by touch or is attempting to pry the wires and tubes from his body, fatigued by medical invasion. Gary seems so tired.

The poem describes this most quotidian hospital visit as divine. Gary as Ganesh, Ganesh as Gary. Gary a deity with "his magical blue trunk, and the dance / of the hands begins again."[17] In the poem's world, the queer in the hospital bed, dying of AIDS, can be divinity itself. The poem sees in his swats a dance, his swollen face a deific semblance. The poem siphons sadness from the gloom of hospitalization, allowing for a different relation to the bedridden body. This is a form of "care work," as K'eguro Macharia terms it—that is, "exhausting and unsexy: cooking and cleaning, visiting hospitals, and planning funerals. Yet, it is this very work of radical interdependence among vulnerable and minoritized groups that multiplies opportunities for survival."[18] I am reminded of lines from Assotto Saint's poem, "Shuffle Along," also about AIDS, also about the time one spends in a hospital when sick. Here a lover documents lying side by side with his lover, a bizarre hospital romance, together dying but together, nonetheless. The lovers are physically connected through the miracle of modern medicine, "hooked up / to the same pole / i.v. garlands" that "strings us / thread-thin yet tight / as life-partners / trapped in this marathon / of disintegration."[19] They share fluids to preserve their bodies a little while longer, like the fluids of the body once shared, cum once enjoyed. Hooked to one another in the morbid dance of death's imminence, both satisfied, as much as they can be, by the thought they will go into what comes next together. The drip-drop of the IV bag their hope, their doomsday clock.

During another scene of hospitalization in *A Dialogue on Love*, Sedgwick in Durham receives a voice message from Fisher in a

Berkeley hospital: "And says he loves me and he wishes things had been different so there would have been more chance to show it." Her immediate aside, to herself, to Fisher who will never be able to read it: "(Though he does show it.)"[20]

I can't find any poems by Sedgwick about Muñoz.

Fisher begins his diary entry for May 4, 1987 with "... On telling Eve Sedgwick that I (think I) have ARC:"—the then-common term for AIDS—immediately following the colon with, "Well, I've told her and now I'm freed up to write, to let loose on the wonder and... words, words gone... it's horrible, just horrible that I should find enjoyment here."[21] He omits from the record how exactly he told her, no details coming after the colon he provides. He must have been behind on his work, must have owed her some writing. Sedgwick, in the afterword to *Gary in Your Pocket*, reports that he had disclosed his status to her in March of that year after having missed several classes, although Fisher dates the disclosure as happening in May. "It wasn't commonplace back then," she writes, "to hear from young people that the futures they look forward to are so modest in duration."[22] She too omits the specifics of his disclosure. As if both had agreed not to do so. In a book chock-full of overexposure, it's fascinating that they both withheld this story. Fisher teasing us with anticipatory punctuation, with that ellipsis leading in—"... On telling Eve Sedgwick that I (think I) have ARC:" It suggests a story to come but amounts to nothing more than a dead-end colon. Perhaps what came after the colon is too unbearable to retell.

The extent of the social differentials between Sedgwick and Fisher become especially clear in the therapist notes that are woven through *A Dialogue on Love*. One reads: "Presentation of Gary's materials at two conferences over the weekend reminds E that she is the wrong person to be promoting this material." The therapist goes on to list Sedgwick's expressed anxieties over being in charge of the materials (her being white, straight, the history of white women serving as patrons of Black writers during the Harlem Renaissance). The therapist continues: "However, she feels she has always been the wrong person to do things she has done professionally and has some investment in making that work, or in demonstrating the interest of that border-crossing position. She identifies it as 'Kosofsky' in some way and relishes the accomplishment."[23]

Sedgwick, in the afterword to *Gary in Your Pocket*, remarks on the process of editing the manuscript: "Almost every night of it I have dreamed, not *of* Gary, but *as* him—have moved through one and another world clothed in the restless, elastic skin of his beautiful idiom."[24] The meaning of this sentence is slippery. Is it Fisher's literary style that fuels Sedgwick's dreaming? Or is the "idiom" she invokes more figurative, a combination Fisher as she knew him, Fisher according to his writing, and Fisher as she imagines him to be? Sedgwick's dream is one of intimacy. It is closeness, nearness to another, the Other. Her editorship allows her to have this intimacy, where Fisher's words transmogrify her into Fisher, her student.

I guess there's something about Fisher's life in the fast lane—his prioritizing of sex and pleasure—that would be alluring to an academic like Sedgwick. Academia guarantees a slower life, has dullness meeting you at every corner. A life of semesters that feel unending. Of waiting for scholarly journals to decide if you will be published or not. Of committee meetings and faculty workshops and routine work squabbles. Fisher's notebooks must have been like a hit of poppers upon Sedgwick's first read. The rush of his prose a fantastic fantasy interjected into the humdrum of the everyday. I am reminded of one Sedgwick's famous axioms, found in the introduction to her 1990 book, *Epistemology of the Closet*: "Many people have their richest mental/emotional involvement with sexual acts that they don't do, or even don't *want* to do."[25]

I don't dream about Muñoz. To be fair, I hardly ever remember any of my dreams come morning. I would like to dream about him, as I would like to dream about others, about those family members no longer in this earthly realm. I only see them in my sleep once or twice a year, if I'm lucky. Dreams like real life, where they become close to me again.

For more than a decade now I've been reading and rereading Muñoz's work, yet he is ever the elusive figure to me. I cannot figure out how to induce the transformation, the becoming-Other, that Sedgwick experienced with Fisher. It seems nice. Becoming someone else, for a little while. Having the freedom to explore the world as they did. But I don't know if I necessarily want this immersion that Sedgwick describes. Maybe I like the apartness. The being able to touch through distance.

According to Fisher's diary entry of May 19, 1993, Flannery O'Connor's lupus "crippled her but also drove her like a fast car," which, he finds, his AIDS does not do. I don't think he's entirely right about this. Even through bouts of intense illness and hospital stays his writing is vibrant, spiraling, pellucid syntax that holds nothing back. Addressing his mentor, he writes that he wishes he could be as creatively inspired as O'Connor: "Eve, I would take opium (not tincture of opium which they're giving me here at the hospital for diarrhea—black in a hospital with bed with a 300,000 dollar view of a white limousine and no dictionary) to drive that fast and that sporty, that loving and that armageddon-bent. I wouldn't mind dying like her if I'd already lived with a conviction that strong."[26]

How did Sedgwick feel when Fisher addressed her in his notebooks? When the student reached out postmortem to the mentor, the teacher who will keep his words alive. Not haunted, not saddened, maybe encharmed. Held.

"I've always been paralyzingly frightened of losing people I love," confesses Sedgwick in *A Dialogue on Love*. She lists the names of those she most fears losing, "the people with whom my empathy's root-deep." Among the names we find Muñoz. Her "José."[27]

3

A few more buttons are done up this time, the shirt dark blue. The collar opened up slightly, at ease, the sleeves rolled up. No sign of an undershirt. It is 2011 and he is on a panel at Barnard College, celebrating his friend and fellow queer theorist Lauren Berlant's newly published book, *Cruel Optimism*. Muñoz takes Berlant's thesis of cruel optimism—"a relation of cruel optimism exists when something you desire is actually an obstacle to your flourishing,"[28] as Berlant phrases it—and puts it into dialogue with his new writing on queer utopianism and the photography of Mark Morrisroe. He honors Berlant's thinking by showing how their thought shapes his new ideas. "Even though its presence threatens their well-being, because whatever the *content* of the attachment is, the continuity of its form provides something of the continuity of the subject's sense of what it means to keep on living on and to look forward to being in the world."[29] As of this writing, this paper on Morrisroe has yet to be published. It's just a presentation given on a panel in 2011. A Muñozian thought I experience for the first time as a video, as the theorist speaking his ideas to me.

He is less animated than his 2003 self. He sits composed behind the table, reading his paper. No more of the lectern grasping or triangulated elbows or pacing about. He doesn't joke around like his 1998 suit-jacketed self, either. He sprinkles a little humor here and there in the presentation, but his attitude is strictly business this evening. The occasion doesn't necessarily call for his 2003 or 1998 self, but you can see how he is now more comfortable in his role as the theorist. He knows what he is doing. He has published two books. He sees how his theories and concepts may address even his friend's work, and has new texts and queer archives to analyze. In his element. Sleeves rolled up, down to business.

Each panel or lecture across the years gives me a different Muñoz. I'm trying to keep up with them all.

Throughout Muñoz's writings, Lauren Berlant is referenced, cited, engaged. They did panels together, some of them recorded, kept in circulation online. He valued their friendship so highly that he would even, at times, cordially disagree with his friend's arguments—a high compliment. In a review of Berlant's 1997 book, *The Queen of America Goes to Washington City*, Muñoz made this point: "While [Berlant's] readings are always engaging and I am convinced and persuaded by most of them, I do not need to be won over by them to be hailed and inspired by the theory they evidence."[30] I admire this sentiment, that friendship does not mean agreement or total acceptance of your friend's ideas. That there can be appreciation for the thinking undertaken, the analytical perspective applied, without necessarily signing off on it. That their thought is fascinating but you're not entirely sure about all of it.

However, I do not take Muñoz here to be merely repeating the facile idea—oft-repeated and widely circulated in neoliberal countries like the United States—that we can uncritically respect differences of opinion. That we should all respect even those opinions that seek your exclusion, your violation, your exploitation, your suffering, and, yes, sometimes, even your death. That violent rhetoric and fantasies of violence are innocent speculations, mere words that can't do anything. Just opinions. Opinions that transmogrify into oppressive policies, border wall constructions, book bans, white nationalist terror and anti-trans panic, school shootings and overseas bombings of non-white populations. Opinions that justify inflicting pain on others. The truth is that we cannot calmly respond, or be expected to calmly respond, to "opinions" that yearn for our annihilation. Opinions are never just opinions in the globally connected world we live in.

Muñoz, in his review of his friend's book, offers a way of rethinking "differences of opinion." We can respect the differing ideas of those who do the research, who do not seek to reproduce structural oppression or systemic violence, who do not traffic in willful ignorance or purposeful oversight. We can, he suggests, respect the ideas of those folks that actually do the reading, where the means may be different than our own, the tools used and strategies divergent, but the ends the same: a different kind of world, a better world, a world unlike this one. An idea with the intent of meaningful change for all is the only kind worth one's salt.

"Lauren has a great capacity to attend to the brutality that we endure in the present," Muñoz said at the Barnard College panel. "When reading the work I picture [Berlant] hunkering down in the foxhole of the here and now, while I'm quick to look for an exit sign in the form of a mostly rhetorical futurity."

After Sedgwick's passing, people reached out to Berlant offering condolences, believing they had been one of Sedgwick's students. "She wasn't technically," Berlant corrected them, "she was my brainstorming friend—although 'storming' isn't quite right, it was more like brain-nudging, the way cats push at legs."[31]

"This chapter is dedicated to José Esteban Muñoz, who kind of hated it when he heard it—'It's not my favorite of your papers . . . ,'" reports Berlant in their posthumously published book, *On the Inconvenience of Other People*. Muñoz's forthrightness regarding the work of his fellow queer theorist is admirable. It seems difficult, at least from my view, to be so blunt in one's evaluation of a friend's ideas. The knuckle punch of a resounding "not my favorite." But changing one's mind is always possible, if, that is, one has enough humility to be wrong from an initial assessment, if one is open to the seduction of liking something one thought they wouldn't like if only experienced in a different way. "[Muñoz] liked it more when he read it, and who pushed me to sustain the motive of its initial vision, which was to address how the impossibility of distinguishing being known and unknown in attachment affects the shape of revolutionary thought."[32]

......

In the same 2011 panel, Muñoz broke from his paper presentation to mention how he had been solicited to write on Morrisroe. However, the theorist said, "I started to worry about the predictability of the kinds of sense I'm asked to make of objects." He did not elaborate further, instead calling the aside an instance of "auto damnation mode," asserting that he was "not interested in recanting my way of doing things," and quickly returning to his presentation. I take his aside here to mean that readers associated him with particular kinds of queer performers and archives (gender bending, in-your-face), and ways of reading them, and therefore wanted his ideas and approaches with regard to other similar subjects. He was expressing, I think, an interest in challenging himself as a thinker and expanding his intellectual repertoire, allowing himself more than "the predictability of the kinds of sense I'm asked to make of objects" without forsaking his interpretative practices and focuses of inquiry. His posthumous book *The Sense of Brown* would certainly branch out in a different critical direction, undertaking a more expansive and deeper theorizing on Latinidad. I assume that, like so many of us who write and publish, he didn't want people to think him predictable, to know ahead of time what texts he would discuss, what he would say about them, and how he would say it. Unless you're Stephen King or Nora Roberts, being thought predictable is an insult. The element of surprise the innovator's pursuit.

But there is something fascinating, too, about the return to what one does best, to excavating moments of unpredictability in the predictable. Returning, after all, is never the same return. Here is Muñoz describing a self-portrait by Morrisroe: The queer artist, he says, "is in the persona of one of his drag characters, Sweet Raspberry. In relatively sharp focus, he looks back at the camera, his head slanted, a jacket falling over his shoulder, face and pearls receding into a larger lagoon of shadows that includes his dark wig that enfolds it." Muñoz's lush description emanates from my computer screen, similar to others across his oeuvre, but also unlike them because this one is not read from a page but heard in his voice. He sounds slightly meek—no poetic theatricality like his friend, Fred Moten, no shy, chirpy articulations like his mentor, Sedgwick—with a light lisp that entrances. The video shows him seated in the bottom left of the screen, enveloped in a murkiness, the result of insufficient lighting at the event. The photograph he describes is projected behind him on a screen for the live audience there that day on April 12, 2011, and for the twenty-six thousand viewers on YouTube that have accumulated a good fifteen years later. The photograph projected on the screen radiates a radioactive yellow, the camera cutting off the top of it. Sweet Raspberry looks back at the viewer with what appears to me to be a kind smile. "Sweet Raspberry, Spanish Madonna" (1986). The original photograph, now in the possession of the Whitney Museum, and available to view online, has no such harsh yellow tint, nor the smile for that matter. It does have a bronze-like color distortion effect in the background, which probably explains the yellowish wash in Muñoz's projection. The rouge-red lips I thought I'd seen smile are instead pressed tightly together, the surrounding skin powdered garishly white, a resting bitch face personified. The "larger lagoon of shadows" Muñoz describes is there in the foreground, surrounding the portraited subject. Seductively, dead seriously, Sweet Raspberry stares at the viewer, her wig in a possible state of movement. It's hard to tell. The textures are blurred together, the colors faded. The year 1986 feels long ago, as does 2011. Yesterday only ever receding further and further away.

The sumptuous phrase "a larger lagoon of shadows": as if anyone who dares look upon that photograph from now on must also hear that arrangement of descriptors, as if the photo can no longer exist without Muñoz's line, as if the photo never was without him, that lagoon of shadows hugging Sweet Raspberry, time speeding on by making the photographic darkness darker, shadowy indistinctions, an embraced collapsing of epochal markers.

. . . . . .

Berlant, in an essay memorializing Muñoz published in *Social Text* in 2014, includes a screenshot of a text message they received from the theorist on February 13, 2013: "Of course things persist. So many people only know there [sic] lives as strung through persistence. Only the lucky few get to argue agonist [sic] the fact of persistence." We don't know the context in which the message was sent—just that he was theorizing on persistence to his friend and colleague. Perhaps in relation to a mutual, or as an offering of wisdom to Berlant, who may have needed it that day. Maybe one of them had reached out to brainstorm an idea—text-message theorizing. I suppose the "agonist" in the text message is a typo, a common occurrence in this hyper-textual online world, like the incorrect use of "there" instead of "their." Most likely he meant to say "against," but "agonist" presents its own tantalizing lexical deviation. Deriving from the Greek word *agon*, meaning conflict or struggle, an agonist is a person who struggles to win or overcome. Persistence can be defined similarly: a struggle on behalf of something, an aspiration to overcome obstacles in pursuit of a goal. People persist, but also, as Muñoz emphasizes, "things persist." The world carries on, even in the aftermath of a loved one's death. It must, and we must too—in the face of loss, in the face of the premature deaths that are all too common among queers, non-white people, and other marginalized folks. We must, even when confronted with overwhelming loss and injustice. We persist as agonists in a world that would rather we not be.

Berlant responds, "I know."

Morrisroe in drag as Sweet Raspberry looks like John Leguizamo in drag as Chi-Chi Rodriguez in the 1995 film *To Wong Foo, Thanks for Everything! Julie Newmar.* Patrick Swayze, Wesley Snipes, and Leguizamo in drag for two hours of comedic genius. A favorite movie of mine. I wonder if Muñoz also saw this similarity.

The theorist had some choice words about films like *To Wong Foo, Thanks for Everything! Julie Newmar*, and about celebrity drag queens like RuPaul. In *Disidentifications* he writes, "Commercial drag presents a sanitized and desexualized queer subject for mass consumption. Such drag represents a certain strand of integrationist liberal pluralism."[33] He identified a '90s-era boom in popular depictions of drag, intended to "hopefully lead to social understanding and tolerance," yet at the same time queers and their civil rights were under all kinds of attack. Things don't look too different twenty years later, in the age of drag brunches, ever more country-specific iterations of *RuPaul's Drag Race*, and the complete mainstreaming of drag in popular culture. Muñoz reflected on the appropriation of hip-hop into other popular forms like musical theater, finding saliency for what has happened to drag: "When de-historized," he wrote, such depictions "can easily become weak multicultural window-dressing passing for actual political representation."[34]

4

The theorist wears a gray sweater, a black collared shirt poking out from the neckline. Comfy, cozy. Slightly less casual than some of his 2000s appearances. He looks like a tenured professor of philosophy, or economics. He looks like he should be a hosting a PBS evening special. He looks like someone you'd want to hang out with for a happy hour cocktail. This type of ensemble appears to be his go-to outfit for lectures and presentations in the final years of his life, as seen across the various recordings and images of him. In this video, filmed in March of 2013, Muñoz is being hosted by *JNT: Journal of Narrative Theory* to present a paper on the topic of the queer commons, alongside Samuel R. Delany. They are the honored guests of the evening. Muñoz reads excerpts from his manuscript for *The Sense of Brown* and plays clips from Wu Tsang's 2012 film *Wildness*, which he analyzes in his book. The film documents the story of the Silver Platter, a queer and trans Latinx bar in Los Angeles. The video of the event seems informally done. Someone recording on their phone from the rafters of the auditorium, perhaps, probably a student. You can barely hear anything, even though he's speaking into a microphone. Whatever he says, though, we know it is of consequence. He's the seasoned theorist by now: presenting papers on his new research, drafting up his third book, ready to formulate a theory explicitly wedding queerness and Latinidad. A long way from the thirty-year-old sporting a suit jacket, honoring his mentor. Here he is in his prime, rocking the gray sweater, black collar out. Relaxed in thought.

"The Sense of Watching Tony Sleep" is a brief yet ineffable essay, originally published in 2007 in a special issue of *South Atlantic Quarterly* dedicated to sex and queer theory, and later republished in a 2011 anthology that expanded upon that issue. Despite the stated theme of the issue and anthology, though, the essay contains little discussion of sex. Instead, the theorist ruminates on his friend, the artist Tony Just, and a series of sketches called *Tony Sleeping*, made by his former lover, Elizabeth Peyton. The theorist sees a kind of queer particularity that arises from the softness and feminineness depicted in these sleepy sketches, even though a heterosexual dynamic defines the portraits. "Sleep, like sex and alongside sex," he writes, "gives us a sense of the world which potentially interrupts practices of thought that reify a kind of ontological totality—a totality that boxes us into an intractable and stalled version of the world."[35] His meditation on sleep, which he terms a "soft emotion," allows him to explore the possibility of moving beyond identity essentialisms—the fixed notions about identities that we so often cling to in order to make sense of the world. He challenges them by reading queer longings in Peyton's drawings that map queerness onto depictions of post-heterosexual-sex napping. He roves across a series of other texts, excavating, for instance, how queer desire operates in Shakespeare's sonnets through a faith in the performative: a doing, rather than an ontological being. The sonnets perform queer desire through subtext and suggestion rather than pronouncing it outright, rather than identifying a relation as queer and, therefore, real and legitimate. "Doing away with feminism, queerness, and race as epistemological certitudes would open a site of potentiality where these particularities exist as methodologies that free new meaning."[36] In short, Muñoz's argument is that we can't know ahead of time what we seek to know. We should not assume that we can anticipate what a term like *queerness* or *feminism* is supposed to mean, or how it is to mean. Something like queerness can take shape in unexpected forms, in the unlikeliest places, and that is what allows it to have a critical edge. Berlant provides another angle: "Queer, socialist/anti-capitalist, and feminist work has all been about multiplying the ways we know that people have lived and can live, so that it would be possible to take up any number of positions during and in life in order to have 'a life.'"[37]

Maybe Muñoz didn't have much to say specifically about sex and queer theory. Unlike his mentor Sedgwick—who openly discussed the literary anality of writers like Henry James, and the masturbatory aesthetics in Jane Austen's work, or even her own exploration of BDSM practices like spanking—Muñoz didn't talk about the nitty-gritties of sex very much. Especially not from his own sex life. Perhaps he just didn't want to talk about sex with the rest of us. I didn't need him to, anyway. The theorist has a right to their privacies.

When depressed, I like to nap. I lay my head on the pillow, close my eyes, and doze off. Sometimes for hours, sometimes for minutes, at any point during the day. My boyfriend comments on how I can nap as many times as I like and still, somehow, sleep through my normal sleep cycle. The insomniac's wet dream.

"I often encounter people who think that 'real' theory is philosophy while queer theory involves moralizing identity performances dressed up as thinking," writes Berlant. "This position strikes me as anti-intellectual, and need I say it, sexually anxious."[38]

I write about my own sex life occasionally. I first started to in order to better understand my lovers. To approach them in a way—distanced, abstracted a bit—that allowed me to understand who they were, what made them tick. When writing about them I thought about the politics of New York City, what neighborhood they lived in, their race, who they lived with, what their place was more broadly in the United States. I wanted to put them in context with what few details I knew of them. Arranging a puzzle with barely any pieces to work with.

So many of them I only knew as sexual partners. There was never any romance, and not really any friendship. I wanted it this way, and most of them did, too. Just because you are erotically compatible does not mean you are romantically compatible. A lesson I learned the hard way from my first dating forays. I mistook sexual chemistry for affection, for a semblance of love. What we did in the bedroom did not necessarily constitute anything more outside the bedroom. This is not to say I didn't care for these lovers. I wanted no harm to come their way. I helped them as I could, if they asked. But it was a relief to have no social or emotional expectations from them. In a life crowded with friends, family, and romantic partners, being able to hang with another human solely inside the bedroom was a godsend.

I write about these familiar erotic strangers in the third person. I inspect them, and my relation to them, from various vantage points. Give them a history, motives for the actions I know about. Biographize. Craft my own private profiles of who I think them to be. Who I think us to be, together.

I nap when I'm not depressed, too. The naps just feel better during bouts of melancholia.

My profiles: my projections of the lovers. Images of fantasy. Getting to know them in my mind's eye.

In Muñoz's oeuvre, the closest we get to a sense of sex and the theorist is a moment in a relatively overlooked article titled "Rough Boy Trade." Published in a 1998 anthology on photography, the piece examines white trade as queer desire in the photography of the straight-identified Larry Clark. Muñoz takes a deep dive into the butch white boys at the center of many of Clark's photographs. They place guns in their mouths as if providing fellatio to the barrels; women circulate in the periphery as buffers (beards?), to negate any queer readings or homosexual assumptions one may (one does) place on the images. In his introductory paragraph, Muñoz provides some anecdotal theorizing on his relation to white boys. "Before I learned to value the beauty of other men of color, white boys held my rapt attention," the theorist confesses—especially, he writes, because of their unavailability to him. "Thankfully they are now only a component of my desire, one of a few types; but still, the fantasy holds. *I am held.*"[39] The semicolon in Muñoz's formulation holds me. Though these white boys may be inaccessible, though they may despise your queerness, they still exert a hold. Fantasy holds, and excites.

In the next paragraph, we find Muñoz pointing an accusatory finger at his peers: "I know I'm not the only one for whom this is true. Dirty white boys, straight-acting and *tradey* white boys still hold a central place in the visual imagination of gay men of all colors, all over the world."[40] He isn't wrong. Almost thirty years after this writing, the queer community still grovels after whiteness. Clone culture is as alive as it was in the 1970s. White queers are synonymous with the entire category of queer, representationally overrepresented. We are primed by the culture writ large to idolize and desire white bodies—it's not just queers, mind you. Muñoz's comment hints at why he so ardently championed queer of color aesthetics and life. He saw the need to stress that his work was not just queer theory but queer of color theory. That these distinctions helped articulate the social and political differences across the queer community. That there was something about race and its relation to queerness that needed attending to.

The tongue-in-cheek humor and anecdotal theorizing of "Rough Boy Trade" was published in the same year that Muñoz gave his wit-laced speech in honor of Sedgwick. For the theorist, there was something about that year—being thirty years old? Leaving behind his youthful twenties and his anxiety about being cool, and plunging into his give-no-damn thirties?—that brought out the jokester and the personal erotic. I want to think 1998 was one of his best years. When he was thirty, flirty, and thriving. When a particular side of him became visible—one we don't get to see too often in his works or talks. A Muñoz that is neither entirely public nor wholly private. A Muñoz that may have emerged in some more extended form, if he hadn't died, in another article, a new book. This 1998 theorist and the fascination over the what-could-have-been again, anew.

5

What did he carry in the pockets of his suit jacket that evening in 1998? Mints, possibly, a lip balm to moisturize during his speech? A pen in case he needed to hastily amend a word or two, a scrap of paper with a well wish from a lover he was seeing that year? Perhaps some quarters to call up a friend on the pay phone afterwards. During his ten minutes on the podium, he never reaches for anything. His hands and body stay rather immobile, unlike other later iterations of his public-speaking self. His grandest movement is when he takes a big gulp of water, one that you can hear in the mic, awkwardly. He's unusually stiff during his ode to Sedgwick. Let's blame it on the suit jacket. The starched uniformity inducing discomfort. Not his style.

He more than likely looked forward to taking it off later, at the afterparty, when everyone was celebrating Sedgwick at some nearby bar. He probably danced a number or two in the garment, to inhabit its suave coolness. After that he would have gotten hot and sweaty and would have needed to peel the jacket off, drape it on a nearby chair, leave it crumpled in the corner of a window, forgotten. He would have kept dancing and drinking. Perhaps had a round or two of shots. He would have enjoyed the night out on the town with his friends and colleagues, indulging in a bit of workplace gossip, the latest celebrity scandal, who's sleeping with who. He would have lost track of time, that exquisite losing of oneself in a good time. Fatigue would have set in, however. When the feet throb and the headache looms and all you want to do is hail a cab, pass out in bed. So he would have said his goodbyes, his until-soons, knowing these friends would be dispersing to their respective corners of the world until the next conference, or panel, or bar hangout. In the cab he would have begun to pass out, faintly remembering that he'd started the evening in a suit jacket, faintly recalling that he'd left something in his pocket. Not his keys or wallet—nothing urgently needed—but something. Something from that evening in 1998, honoring his Eve.

V

TURN THE PULSE AROUND

On the morning of June 12, 2016, a Sunday, I woke up in my Manhattan apartment to see several missed calls and voice messages from my mother. "I need to know where you are," her first message started out. "I saw on the news what happened. Please call me back." When I called her back, she picked up and sighed deeply. "Oh, thank god. I know you just like to pick up and leave without giving anyone notice. I thought you could have been there. In Orlando. At Pulse."

My mother seemed to think she was breaking the news to me, but I already knew. I had still been up in the wee hours the night before, when social media accounts began to report the massacre, when concerned texts from friends started coming in. At around 2 a.m., just after last call, twenty-nine-year-old Omar Mateen had entered Pulse nightclub with a semiautomatic rifle. It was Latin Night. He fired. And fired again, and again, round after round, sending bullets into the crowd, into bodies. Into flesh went those bullets. Into the flesh of those plenty who had traveled across the Caribbean and the lower Americas to Orlando from Haiti, Puerto Rico, Cuba, Mexico, and the Dominican Republic. Into the flesh of a mother who would perish protecting her queer child with her body. Into the flesh of singers and hairdressers and nurses and photographers and literature students. Into the flesh those bullets went. Into flesh of those who wanted, for an evening, a few hours, a moment, to be free to move their bodies joyously to the rhythms of Latin Night.

I did not know the details and circumstances of these lives when the news of the massacre was breaking. I just knew, at the deepest of levels, that they were like me: Queers of color, broke queers, queer Latinx people, queer people composed of diasporic rhythms, queers moving across the globe, queers who have had to reckon with worlds hostile and cruel to their being. I found myself already haunted by their deaths, was awestruck at how soon I felt that loss. Haunted by the body counts, the names, the stories and histories attached to those names, like I am haunted by the many thousands of queers both named and unnamed whom we have lost to AIDS. Much as Muñoz describes his search for the late Cuban American artist Ana Mendieta—"What is attempted when one looks for [her]? What does her loss signify in the here and now? More importantly: What comes after loss?"[1]—I too am searching for the dead, for those we lost at Pulse, to AIDS. I am searching for all those names, those fragmented stories, contemplating what it means to be after loss—after Pulse, after the AIDS dead, always in this cruel and devastating *after*.

José Muñoz passed away three years before the Pulse massacre. The most eminent queer Latinx theorist wasn't here to respond to this violence. He was one of the first people I wanted to hear from. His words and thoughts would have been the refuge I needed. But, there and then, all I felt was his absence, as I do now—an absence that is oppressively encompassing and total. What would he have said? And with him gone, how do I search for a response to the unthinkable, the unbearable that was Pulse?

In a 2002 essay responding to the events of 9/11, Muñoz—then teaching at NYU and living in university housing—recounts how he had watched from his balcony as the towers fell. In his account he centers his students: the fact he had to continue working, to change the course material to respond to the events the students were seeing unfold around them. He played for his students *Cornered*, a video by the performance artist Adrian Piper, in which she delivers a monologue on race and racial classification. Muñoz recalls how half of his students "attempted to say something like, 'Now, in this time of tragedy, race does not seem to matter at all.'"[2] But Muñoz identified with the rest of the students, who posited that race matters now more than ever. He tried to mediate all views. That tricky pedagogical balance.

His students' refrain—that there was a time and place for discussing race—is nothing new in the United States. This selective choosing of when and where race matters has been foundational to American culture. "Insisting on the meaninglessness of race to the American identity," as Toni Morrison aptly puts it, "are themselves full of meaning. The world does not become raceless or will not become unracialized by assertion. The act of enforcing racelessness in literary discourse is itself a racial act."[3] Morrison observes how, when race is dismissed as unimportant, this dismissal itself becomes important, speaking to the sensibilities of white tolerance and permissibility. The novelist and critic Jess Row, in an assessment of whiteness within mid-twentieth-century novels, identifies what he calls "white flights," or the ways white writers have practiced a "wishful thinking as a way of life, a way out of seeing, and a way of making art."[4] White identity, culture, and life go unremarked in the work of white writers, whereas the cultures of Black and other non-white writers are always marked by the culture at large. Echoing Morrison's formulation, Row provocatively tells it as it is: "Stories not only deny but undeny, tell but untell themselves."[5] Disavowing not only race, but also white identity and representations of whiteness, is an American pastime.

In the US, the degree to which race matters varies according to the needs of the dominant culture. In the case of 9/11, race—and particularly the racedness of Arab and Muslim peoples both in and out of the US—was especially critical to legitimizing the project of global terror, violence, and mass murder that this nation would commit under the banner of "freedom." Muñoz, in his introduction to a volume of two performances by Coco Fusco that confronted the politics of the post-9/11 US, postulates that "Fusco's performance enacts a kind of hypercamouflage by pushing camouflage's process of naturalizing. The nation's performance of the state of exception, its current Middle East policy, and even its use of words like 'liberation' and 'freedom' are ideological disguises that are meant to be taken as natural."[6] This naturalization of us versus them, West versus The Rest, good guys versus bad guys, makes acceptable extreme forms of violence and suffering for non-white peoples. This is what we saw unfold in Iraq and Afghanistan. Race doesn't matter, so we are made to believe, when discussing mass shootings in the United States—even though they are overwhelmingly committed by radicalized white men with ties to white nativist organizations and white supremacist ideologies. We are repeatedly told by the ruling class that no one "sees" race when it comes to hiring practices, which neighborhoods police terrorize, which schools go underfunded, or which communities go deprived of water or other resources. But race always matters, even when we are told otherwise.

After the killings at Pulse, a particular kind of invocation of race occurred in the mainstream culture, emphasizing the shooter's Arabness and documented allegiance to ISIS. A dominant narrative emerged in which Islamic terrorism was the culprit, protecting US citizens and the US nation-state from outside evils was the priority, and the realities of the queer lives lost became erased. On social media, non-Latinx white queer people subsumed the differences among the people in that club, reducing them to a generic and generalized "queer" identity. In so doing, they erased the urgent specificities: this shooting had occurred on Latin night, a night in which Black Latinx, non-Black Latinx, and African American queer and trans people go to clubs.

At the end of his meditation on teaching in the wake of 9/11, Muñoz speaks to the role of the educator after atrocities: "Pedagogues must offer their students much needed critical tools, practices of thought that will allow them to face the present and embrace a better place and time, a future that is not structured by the violent asymmetries th[at] led to the attack of September 11th and the devastation which followed."[7] To be after Pulse is to be after events like 9/11. Events that sunder holes in the fabric of daily life. Events of cataclysmic horror that require critical tools and language to understand. Otherwise, their meanings can be grafted onto whatever political agendas one sees fit, like the case of Pulse in the immediate aftermath of the shooting. Muñoz saw this as soon as the towers fell in downtown Manhattan. He knew early on the importance of mounting vigilance against the way events like this are put through the US imperialism machine. "Nations provoke fantasy," as Lauren Berlant cogently theorizes.[8] He knew that such events would become battlegrounds of interpretation, with those in power going to great lengths (media manipulation, outright lies, vilifying Muslims and Arabs, war itself) to ensure that their narrative prevailed. His classroom intervention was, no doubt, a small-scale effort to curb these meritless interpretations, but it still mattered. These everyday efforts must mean something. Otherwise, 9/11—and Pulse, and the many other events like them—have meaning only in the malevolently manipulated, abundantly shortsighted, and disastrously destructive ways dictated by those in power.

Forty-nine people were killed at Pulse. Say the number out loud, slowly: forty-nine. They each had a name. Juan Ramon Guerrero. Darryl Roman Burt II. Deonka Deidra Drayton. Antonio Davon Brown. Mercedez Marisol Flores...

"Yesterday we saw ourselves die again // Fifty times we died in Orlando," mourns the narrator of Christopher Soto's poem, "All the Dead Boys Look Like Us." The we—the many colonized, the us, the queer and of color—the poem's plural subaltern voice.

Forty-nine people were killed at Pulse. Many in their twenties, some in their late teens, just babies. Tevin Eugene Crosby. Jonathan

Antonio Camuy Vega. Christopher Joseph Sanfeliz. Yilmary Rodriguez Solivan. Geraldo A. Ortiz-Jimenez…

Richard Blanco, in his own tribute to the Pulse victims, "One Pulse—One Poem," writes: "picture the choir of their invisible spirits / rising with the smoke toward disco lights, imagine / ourselves dancing with them until the very end."[9]

Forty-nine people were killed at Pulse. They were friends and lovers, mothers and siblings and partners and so much more. Alejandro Barrios Martinez. Angel L. Candelario-Padro. Gilberto Ramon Silva Menendez. Akyra Murray. Jason Benjamin Josaphat…

"Restored Mural for Orlando" by Roy G. Guzmán focalizes around the importance of a city like Orlando for queer community. Yet: "I am afraid of attending places / that celebrate our bodies because that's also where our bodies // have been cancelled / when you're brown and gay you're always dying / twice."[10]

The names of the forty-nine go on, as do the details of their lives. Some were professional dancers. Many worked for Disney, one of Orlando's main employers, at some point in their lives. Some sang. Others were devoted fathers. Some were boyfriends, took their final breaths together as boyfriends. One worked at the popular Spanish broadcasting company Telemundo. Another loved Selena Gomez and had come to Orlando to see her in concert….

This mourning is akin to the form of Pedro Pietri's "Puerto Rican Obituary," a poetic eulogy to the Puerto Ricans of the mid-to-late twentieth century. "Juan / Miguel Milagros / Olga / Manuel / All died yesterday today / and will die again tomorrow / passing their bill collectors / on to the next of kin."[11] Pietri, the bard-prophet, articulated the way colonial debt and trauma carry forward. How people with those most common names and most common stories of transnational movement would pay a heavy price, before and after death. How they would die owing and owing. And he anticipated how their next of kin would find themselves at Pulse that evening, dying—as their forebears did—while searching for refuge, for a release from the fetters of the colonial condition. Could Olga—sweet

Olga, who landed in New York City's Lower East Side in the '60s or '70s with a few bucks to her name—have known her child would get gunned down shaking their culo to salsa and hip-hop? Did pious Manuel, who came to New Haven in the '80s to fix cars, foresee his grandchild being killed in an instant under disco lights and sweaty queer bodies? Pietri prophesied their broke asses. Their mundane yet wholly human searches for love and friendship and a future to call their own. Their need to feel that evening the grooves of the Caribbean or Latin America in them, shaking and shimmying and pressing up against their lovers, their lineages, their timelessness.

For so very long, the colonial condition has taken away the lives of those like Milagros and Juan, slowly and ingloriously. Pulse took away so many names and lives in the course of minutes. Since the AIDS epidemic began forty years ago, over seven hundred thousand people have died of the disease and its related complications in the United States. Many of them queer, many of them poor, most of them people of color.

Numbers are hard to process.

In 2018, I visited the P.P.O.W. gallery, where a recreation of David Wojnarowicz's 1990 work *The Lazaretto: An Installation About the Current Status of the AIDS Crisis* was held. Statistics related to HIV/AIDS abounded throughout the installation; a textual and visual aesthetic converged to make the viewer *feel* the weight of numbers. Macabre in style, the installation was mazelike, with walls made of black trash bags. On those walls were white posters with testimonies of people living with AIDS written in black marker. In the center of the installation, a television showed footage from its first iteration, with statistics about AIDS on the surrounding walls. The 2018 recreation was a condensed version of the 1990 original installation, and one of the components omitted was Yvonne's room, which was instead shown on the television footage. The room was based on Wojnarowicz's collaborator Paul Marcus's experience working as an outreach worker for a Bronx clinic, where he met a young Puerto

Rican woman named Yvonne who was living with HIV/AIDS. He helped take care of her for some time, and he also filmed her sharing her thoughts on life and her illness before she passed. Her story inspired the collaboration for the installation. Yvonne's room portrayed a decomposing body lying on a bed, pill bottles and garbage thrown around her. Written on the walls, in what appears to be blood, were injustices done to minoritized peoples by government policies. Marcus recalls that, in 1990, "we had text written in freehand. David and I interviewed people for that. We wrote them in different handwritings, so we would have the sense of different voices and experiences. We wrote them in the languages in which they were told, and some were in Spanish." Their goal was to show the injustices that people living with HIV/AIDS were facing, "dealing with their landlords, getting or not getting on a trial medication, what the role of the government was, what their involvement with the bureaucracies here in the city were, personal experiences between them and their friends. . . . And we covered the walls of this maze with their words."[12] The writing put governmental negligence—and the disposability of deviant bodies—front and center in the original *Lazaretto.*

The combined textual and visual elements of the installation spoke to the weight of numbers. Language met stories met the tally. The art of AIDS is the art of text is the art of the statistic. The realities these kinds of facts and truths express are inseparable from and, as Wojnarowicz's work highlights, constitutive of the process of making art. *Lazaretto* took the statistic from its typical context of grudging realism—the report on a CDC brochure, a presentation at a conference, the five o'clock news—and placed it within the domain of art. There it becomes unfamiliar, perhaps more shocking and appalling. The statistic is potentially more enticing as an installation than as a classroom presentation or public report. It eats away at the sensibility of those who expect art to exist in the abstract, the conceptual, the disembodied, the depoliticized, the art for Art's sake. As one critic has put it: "In keeping with his belief that exposing one's suffering is a political act, this, Wojnarowicz's final installation, brilliantly and persuasively recasts the private sickroom as the scene of a public crime."[13]

Names do not necessarily tell the story of a life, and neither does a number. Yet, when brought together, compiled and compacted, they speak to vast contexts and histories. Forty-nine people killed almost immediately at Pulse. Seven hundred thousand dead—disproportionately poor, unhoused, and people of color—from HIV/AIDS. The hundreds of thousands of Puerto Ricans displaced, exploited, and killed in the name of colonization and enslavement who had names like Juan, Milagros, Olga. The many other names and numbers we will never know because history did not record them. Yet, despite their incompleteness, we need these names and numbers in order to have a sense of our lost, to feel the weight of the tally—not as a burden but as part of our fight for a different past, present, and future. Seeking the stories of a thousand lives in a name, and a thousand histories in a statistic, become our ways of being among the many gone.

According to the World Health Organization, an estimated 3.4 million people have died from the COVID-19 virus. They know this number to be an undercount.

Christopher Soto's memorial to Pulse, "All the Dead Boys Look Like Us," also mentions Muñoz. Unanticipated death and unanticipatable loss link the mass shooting and the theorist's passing. José Esteban Muñoz "Made us feel that queer Brown survival was possible // But he didn't / Survive & now // On the dance floor // in the restroom // On the news // In our chest / There are another // Fifty bodies that look like ours."[14] Muñoz part of the morbid tally, of those "bodies that look like ours," of the innumerable open seasons on queer of color life that take the shape of bullets fired, of medical neglect and governmental disregard of disease, of beatings on the street, of the existential stress itself stopping us in our tracks. All and always an extension of the Pulse mortality count. Of what Pulse has come to symbolize. What Pulse means to *us*.

No consensus exists on what constitutes a mass shooting—each data-gathering agency has different criteria, and as a result, varying statistics on their frequency. According to the Nelson A. Rockefeller Institute of Government of the State University of New York, for instance, "a mass shooting is an incident of targeted violence carried out by one or more shooters at one or more public or populated locations. Multiple victims (both injuries and fatalities) are associated with the attack, and both the victims and location(s) are chosen either at random or for their symbolic value. The event occurs within a single 24-hour period, though most attacks typically last only a few minutes. The motivation of the shooting must not correlate with gang violence or targeted militant or terroristic activity."[15] The Gun Violence Archive defines a mass shooting as simply requiring "a minimum of four victims shot, either injured or killed, not including any shooter who may also have been killed or injured in the incident."[16] The Rockefeller Institute reported that an estimated 441 mass shootings have occurred in the United States between 1966 and 2022, but if you have lived in the US at any point in the twenty-first century, you know this to be a gross undercount. Since the early 2010s, gun violence research organizations have counted hundreds of mass shootings per year. The Gun Violence Archive reported 688 in 2021 alone. Everytown for Gun Safety had a similar figure for that year: 686. The methodologies and data may be different from agency to agency, but the frequency remains despairingly alarming nonetheless—the injuries and death count unspeakably high, thousands upon thousands through the years. The resounding trauma untallyable.

Like Pulse, Hurricane Maria disproportionately harmed Puerto Rican lives. The 2017 hurricane claimed the lives of 4,645 people. Four thousand, six hundred, and forty-five. Say the tally out loud; it devastates.

In 2023, I visited an exhibition at the Whitney Museum titled *no existe un mundo poshuracán: Puerto Rican Art in the Wake of Hurricane Maria*. Borrowing its title from the poetry of Roque Raquel Salas Rivera, the exhibition assembled a broad array of work by Puerto Rican artists responding to Hurricane Maria. The range of the artworks was kaleidoscopic, using Hurricane Maria as a catalyzing nexus to address many interrelated issues: Puerto Rico's longstanding status as a US colony, disaster capitalism, corrupt government, collapsing infrastructure, displacement, and the general disinvestment from and privatization of the archipelago by neoliberal capitalism. One of the works, Gabriella Torres-Ferrer's *Untitled (Valora tu mentira Americana)* (2018), showed a lamppost knocked over during Hurricane Maria, actual disaster detritus, and a sign attached advising Puerto Ricans to value their US citizenship. The destroyed lamppost found symbolic resonance with Puerto Rico's failing electric grid, enduring blackouts in the hurricane's aftermath, and the problem of who would supply the electricity and fund its maintenance. The gritty materiality of the piece made Puerto Rico's infrastructure crisis all the more apparent and tangible, a tangibility sonically echoed in the exhibition's video installation by Elle Pérez, *Blackout* (2022). Pérez documented the constant nighttime moments of darkness during the post-Maria blackouts from a window. Snatches of sound (voices, car engines, trees rustling, frogs) in the darkness remind you that you are not alone: A noise in the distance links you to a network of shared catastrophe and hope, a makeshift intimacy between the humans and nonhumans trying to navigate the post-disaster landscape. Sonic darkness connects an archipelago.

The exhibition *no existe un mundo poshuracán* indexed not only the urgency of the present but also the unresolved urgencies of the past. The painting *Google the Ponce Massacre* (2021), by Danielle De Jesus, depicts victims from the 1937 Ponce Massacre superimposed with a scene from the 2019 protests against then-Governor Ricardo Rosselló. His hateful comments and attempts to sell out the island to foreign investors were leaked, leading to a series of protests throughout the Puerto Rican diaspora demanding his resignation. These actions would come to be known as the *Verano de 19* and would generate the mobilizing hashtag #RickyRenuncia. The foreground of the painting portrays a masked protestor and a cop from the protest held in New York's Union Square, which the artist had attended. Like other works throughout the exhibition, De Jesus's painting shows how past events, histories, and traumas accumulate.

"What would it require to imagine a future beyond this current maelstrom?" asks the curator, Marcela Guerrero, in the exhibition catalog, and many of the artworks address that challenge.[17] Yiyo Tirado Rivera's sandcastle sculpture, *La Concha* (2022), modeled after a beachfront hotel built in 1958, points to the gradual weathering of Puerto Rico's luxury facilities and its economy's dependence on tourism. The inevitable crumbling of the sculpture back into sandy formlessness marks a potential future in which Puerto Rico will be able to start over—in which playgrounds for the foreign rich will not determine the viability of its life and culture. Meanwhile, Gamaliel Rodríguez's magenta drawings, *Figure 1828 LMM* (2018) and *Figure 1829 BQN* (2018), depict airport control towers overtaken by tropical foliage. These images herald a future in which tourism and extraction will not dictate Puerto Rico's autonomy, but also a future without the economic displacement and lack of opportunities that are currently forcing Puerto Ricans to leave their home. In this tropical magenta future, airplanes will be unnecessary, obsolete, a relief to our overwhelmingly overburdened planet. Puerto Rican desires and dreams will be free to fly by other means.

Another piece by Rodríguez, *Collapsed Soul* (2020–21), is a painting showing a ghostly blue cargo ship on the open water. A plume of smoke rises from the ship's middle into the sky—the ship is dead, destroyed. As with the airport control towers, we bear witness to a future without climate-destroying vessels—vessels that currently signal the ongoing impacts of the Jones Act, imperial blockades, maritime border patrols, the trans-Atlantic slave trade, and the colonization of the Caribbean. In Rodríguez's blue future, there are no such vessels in Puerto Rico. What remains is the sea itself, its ebbs and flows freed from the violence and apocalypse of colonial jurisdiction, now a site of possibility for the Puerto Rican people.

The exhibition *no existe un mundo poshuracán* did not shy away from airing the grievances of coloniality. As the artworks evinced, the weight of the colonial condition is heavy, bearing down on the backs of Puerto Ricans who have no choice but to play the role of Atlas. But *no existe un mundo poshuracán* also embodied the insurgent creativity of Puerto Rican peoples—the radical imaginaries offering up archipelagic tactics of resistance, survival, and jubilation. Through generations, through crises, through calamities, the Puerto Rican people persist.

The Guatemalan American poet Maya Chinchilla's "Church at Night," written in honor of Pulse, enacts what Cherríe Moraga and Gloria Anzaldúa have termed "theory in the flesh." "A theory in the flesh," according to the two lesbian Chicana theorists, "means one where the physical realities of our lives—our skin color, the land or concrete we grew up on, our sexual longings—all fuse to create a politic born of necessity."[18] "Church at Night" does just that by bringing in the human everydayness of those forty-nine lost, and of the many others injured. Who knew going to the club could be theory? But it is, as the poem shows us, demonstrating the ways those who voyaged out to Pulse that evening, like Chinchilla, like me, like us, "meet up to get ready, / a few drinks before entry, / to save our dollars for tacos / to soak up the night life in our belly."[19] Tacos after a night out: the pleasurable banality of queer living, an ordinary event so crucial to being together with friends and lovers, so crucial to preventing a hangover, so crucial for doing this thing called living.

Even as the poem honors the glorious ordinariness of the queer club on Latin night, it also shows how Pulse, and the people murdered there that night, were politicized: "The beat remains while they beat our remains / some for political gain / *our thoughts and prayers but nothing else / are with you!*"[20] Through those italics,

Chinchilla incisively invokes how mass shootings in the United States are met not with actionable steps, or actual deep cultural change, but with prayers. Prayers given by regular people, politicians, and notable figures; prayers that do not solve the shootings driven by anti-queerness, misogyny, or white supremacy. The offered prayers merely provide depoliticized sympathy, merely minimize the pain that surrounds mass shootings. "What is the force of praying for something bad not to happen, when it has already happened?" Sedgwick asked in her posthumously published book *The Weather in Proust* (2011), a prescient sentiment for our mass-shooting times.[21] Yet, as Chinchilla shows us, the beat remains, drumming on despite the erasure and cruelty by those who would offer prayers instead of change.

The "beat" in Chinchilla's poem is the beat of the choir at church, the beat of our lost and struggling, and the beat of our church, the queer nightclub. The "beat" is our religion.

"Latin/o bodies serve as the site of a long history of racial, cultural, and economic conflict," write Muñoz and Celeste Fraser Delgado in a cowritten 1997 piece on Latino and Latin American dance practices. "Dance promises the potential reinscription of those bodies with alternative interpretations of that history. Magnificent against the monotonous repetition of everyday oppressions, dance incites rebellions of everynight life."[22]

The day after the massacre, the queer Puerto Rican author Justin Torres published an essay in the *Washington Post* called "In Praise of Latin Night at the Queer Club." It too operates as theory in the flesh. Torres writes not just about the victims but with them, a poetic and theoretical embrace where words become flesh, and flesh becomes transcendence. "Lap the bar, out for a smoke, back inside, the ammonia and sweat and the floor slightly tacky, another drink"—his impressionistic writing caresses, holds you firm. "The imperative is to get loose, get down, find religion, lose it, find your hips locked into another's, break, dance on your own for a while—but you didn't come here to be a nun—find your lips pressed against another's, break, find your friends, dance."[23] But the writing also swings us across to the ever-real reality of our histories, of what traumas these bodies bear: "You have known violence. You have known violence. You are queer and you are brown and you have known violence." Yes. That.

Chinchilla and Torres not only lift those at Pulse into poetic transcendence, but they do so for all of us who see ourselves in that night. The capacious us that is queers of color, queer Latinx folks, and transnational and hemispheric peoples. Our everyday clubbing a divine experience.

What is even more profound is that neither writer includes a phrase like "That could have been me." They could have easily done that, could have used such a phrase to project interest or urgency upon the event in terms of its proximity to us. If it could have been *me* that died but *I* didn't, there is a lesson to be learned here and importance to extol upon the event. Though innocently stated, the pronouns in such formulations suggest that we need a tragedy to be related to us in order to care deeply and fully.

Why do we need to see ourselves in the horrific in order to account for its importance? Admittedly, my first reaction to Pulse when it happened in 2016 was to lean into that phrase and its proximity to me. That was why I began writing this chapter: I saw myself in Pulse and needed to speak on it. However, after years of rereading Torres's essay and Chinchilla's poem, struggling to get at what *exactly* I had to say, I noted how both writers simultaneously did and didn't see themselves in Pulse. They highlighted the social differences (race, nationality, citizenship status) that constitute categories like *Latinx*, *queer*, and *queer of color*. These categories are not monoliths and hail a plurality of experiences. These two writers did not speak on behalf of any of these groups but attended to the many types of lives, histories, and realities that congregated at an Orlando queer club—their church—for an evening. Rather than traffic in cohesion, uniformity, and reduction, they sought nuance, specificity, and multiplicity.

When we believe that we need to see ourselves in a tragedy in order to care about it, this clouds our ability to mobilize broadly, passionately, and committedly on behalf of those unlike us. I don't need to see myself in the four little Black girls who were mercilessly bombed and murdered at a Birmingham church in 1963 in order to care about the death-giving machinations of anti-Black violence. I don't need to see myself in the thousands upon thousands of Iraqis murdered by US troops to know that the US nation-state has thrived off terrorizing and exploiting racialized peoples across the globe. I don't need to see myself in the tens of thousands of Maya Indigenous people killed by the Guatemalan government in the final decades of the twentieth century, massacred and disappeared for land, resources, and the glory of having a settler colonial nation. I don't need to see myself…

There is no shortage of examples. I could move across locations, times, and peoples. For some I know many of the facts, and for some I don't know any. For some situations the facts can be looked up, and for others the tallies are impossible to find or have been obscured to hide their gravity. What I know for certain is that global anti-Blackness, extractive capitalism, Islamophobia, misogyny, anti-trans violence, and Indigenous genocide, among so many other violent social forces, shape our planet. I know they exist. I know they manifest in their particularity. I know I must continue to research and learn about them. And, above all else, I know that the many types of people who have been harmed by these forces—in locations and times different from my own, with political and social realities different from mine—matter.

My suspicion is that the need to see oneself in an event in order to care about it is precisely why white supremacy reigns so forcefully and openly in the United States. White people have rarely seen themselves as the victims of state-mandated bombings, or as peoples weighed down by racism or coloniality. Therefore, they do not need to care all that much to end these institutionalized logics, harms, and systems. 9/11 provides an interesting case study of what happens when white people, in a large enough number, are violently killed. White America *saw* itself in those crumbling towers. In a televised instant, they saw the heights and successes of their empire, their conquests and ideologies, collapse. The response by the US government was swift, and devastating. Agents of the state went out to the Middle East to torture, impoverish, injure, and kill in the name of "security," "peace," and "freedom." The white citizens of the United States saw themselves so frighteningly reflected in the events of 9/11 that they had to react with the violent tactics so familiar to them and their ancestors—with guns, batons, pepper spray, and bombs—in order to maintain the legitimacy and supremacy of their global grip, their choke hold.

The answer is not to make white people care by committing violence against them. Nor is my intention to undermine the power of marginalized peoples mobilizing around events in which they see themselves. The point I am making is simple: we need to open up more avenues to caring better, to empathizing more deeply, to fighting for others who are not like us. I do not move in the world as my father does—my father who is dark brown and I who am not—though we share the same blood and common history, though we are both Mexican and Indigenous descendants. How do we get those who are unlike us to understand, to rally, to change the very foundations of our societies? How do we assemble against the cruel logics, rationales, and policies that we have never experienced firsthand but are far too real, far too prevalent, for those we may know or, more likely, never know?

When I lectured on Chinchilla's poem and Torres's essay in a remote course I was teaching, I choked up in front of the computer screen of students. Let me clarify: I choked up and did not cry. I make this distinction not out of some masculinist motivation, nor for fear of being seen as vulnerable or, even more crudely, sentimental. The significance I place upon having choked up—throat constricting and drying up, eyes welling up with tears but not releasing them, mind losing the ability to gather thoughts and speak properly—was that it spoke to the awe-inducing nature of Moraga's theory in the flesh. In that moment I felt those forty-nine not solely as a number, or as a news report, or as a list of names, but as literature. I was choked up not from effusive emotion but from my body being halted, undramatically and unincredibly, by the writings.

I now know that this seizing of my body was a transcendent experience. An experience induced by the metaphors, italics, adjectives, enjambment, style, and other accoutrements of literary language, carefully composed. Transcendence informed by the everyday happenings of queer nightclubbing, queer pleasure-seeking, queer euphoria. I sensed the divine entering me, overcoming me as I lectured. I could not speak. I could not order my thoughts. My transcendence occurred in part because I was critically relishing the plethora of mundane yet exacting details that Chinchilla and Torres had summoned—those details that define going out to the club, that evoke the scope and scale of the crowd at Latin night. That's what Latin night is all about—the messiness of queer life. Being in skin-to-skin proximity with those who are both like and unlike you. Hips and asses thrown around with a reckless abandon full of care, with an attention to the surrounding bodies who we want so desperately to press up against, who we hope want to press up against us. The pressing-up frees us from the injustices outside. Latin night is about the thriving of differences among the various groups and communities that it hails. It is about being brought together to feel and move and sense our queerness as a racially experienced phenomenon. Muñoz, writing on punk rock, describes its power in words that could also apply to Latin night. It "is about inelegantly cutting and stitching a sense of the world together; it is about imagining a commons that is held together by nothing more than a safety pin."[24] I felt all this, that day lecturing before my computer, all at once in the seizing of my body: like church at night, the drumming up of some inexplicably discernible glory, our safety-pinned commonness rising rhythmically to the beat of the evening, the soundscapes of oceans and borderlands and the Caribbean, the living pulse of our multitudes, our riotous resurrections under disco light.

Let me return, one last time, to Muñoz's account of teaching in the aftermath of 9/11. Or, more specifically, I want to turn to the inciting incident for his writing the piece: How he had been *there* to witness those towers fall. How he was on his balcony watching when the towers collapsed, and how he knew "many of [his] students watched from their dorms."[25] Unlike a mass shooting or an epidemic, the scene unfolded at a scale that could be witnessed by both a theorist on his balcony and by television viewers around the world. A spectacle. Not censored from the news because, as vulgar as it sounds, it was like a science fiction movie. The human suffering masked by the size of the towers and the planes, by the sheer magnitude of it. Unreal, unimaginable. Like Muñoz, like his students, we were all spectators to the horror.

With Pulse, as well as with the HIV/AIDS epidemic, I don't know if we can have such a relation. There is no way one could have been a spectator in these situations. Some have survived mass shootings or epidemics, yes, but they weren't spectators. They were part of the horror. Those horrors are lived. Trying to represent Pulse, or HIV/AIDS, both of which disproportionately impacted people of color, would be different than representing 9/11. Intolerably more horrendous.

To be *after* Pulse, to be *after* HIV/AIDS, then, can only mean being after a patchwork of lives lived, news reports, statistics, names, photos, and the art and writings we make to be with those we've lost. Pulse is the theorist on the balcony, contemplating and feeling, figuring out how to teach and study in the aftermath of a horrendous event. Pulse is my mother thinking I was dead when she called me after the massacre, again and again. It is her thinking I had become a number, a statistic, a news report, another queer dead and gone, much what she'd experienced with her queer brother. I had not become another queer number.

My mother called me after Pulse because she knew something of tragedy, mourning, and fear. But in truth her attitude toward me has been inflected by that cocktail of emotions long before that terrible morning, ever since I elected to move to New York City when I was eighteen. They are the feelings one gives to a queer child. Fear of our early passing from some disease, some mental illness, some lover's quarrel, some brutal attack by a stranger on a street. Our queer tragedy emanating through the lives of those we knew.

Muñoz, positing on the queerness of punk rock, writes that "to want more is to desire an enhancement of our multiple senses of the world."[26] I want Pulse not to be solely a tragedy, a massacre, a mass shooting. I want it to signify more than pain, suffering, and unending mourning. I want *after* Pulse to be about the patchwork of joys, contradictions, mundanities, hopes, differences, and freedom projects that define queer life. The many ways of reaching out with all of our senses to other bodies, other places, other histories. The after that is queers shaking asses, gossiping with friends while nursing cocktails, lip-syncing to a favorite song, staring into the strobe lights feeling alive, fully bodied, transcendent. After Pulse is where I want to be. In that wanting that is wanting more, *after* all this.

VI

SAINT MUÑOZ

1. AFTERLIVES IN BROWN

Chanting, cackling, shouting, and frolicking up Manhattan's Sixth Avenue, flaunting our booty shorts and glittered skin, we marched. It was June 2019, and thousands of us queers were having a grand old gay time at the first Queer Liberation March. The march was held the same day as the yearly Pride parade, in protest against that corporatized, sanitized bigger event. At the Liberation March were anti-capitalists, gender deviants, anarchists, kink-positive folks, Marxists, and all other stripes of queer radicals. This was the parade for me.

People brought all kinds of posters to the march. Short, sweet signs with punchy messaging. Verbose signs that required extensive parsing. Signs that lambasted various local, national, and international political figures for their homophobia, transphobia, racism, classism, and sexism, rightfully so. There were many posters of Sylvia Rivera and Marsha P. Johnson, giving them recognition so well-deserved. Karl Marx made cameos among the signs, as did Michel Foucault—the marchers had Photoshopped the faces of these two thinkers into their own unique designs and messages. The posters were a sea—too many to take in, to be honest. Yet, out of the corner of my eye, I spotted him, deified, his head enshrouded in a globe of light, bobbing up and down, his papery two-dimensionality held up in the air by an unseen marcher. I couldn't believe it! Here was Muñoz on Sixth Avenue, a queer icon among other icons. The marcher had used the photo of the turtlenecked Muñoz, staring seriously ahead, a wall of books behind him. Middle-aged Muñoz, Muñoz the seasoned theorist. I nudged my friend next to me, alerting him of this appearance. My friend—not an academic, not one to read the latest theory churned out by a university press—replied, "Oh cool. But who is he?"

A year after that first Queer Liberation March, and a mere few months after the onset of the COVID-19 pandemic, Muñoz's final monograph, *The Sense of Brown*, was posthumously published. I had first encountered excerpts of Muñoz's unfinished project—originally titled *Feeling Brown*—in 2014, during my first semester of doctoral study. We were assigned two Muñoz articles that he'd written as part of this larger project on Latino identity: "Feeling Brown: Ethnicity and Affect in Ricardo Bracho's *The Sweetest Hangover (and Other STDs)*" (2000) and "Feeling Brown, Feeling Down: Latina Affect, the Performativity of Race, and the Depressive Position" (2006). The 2000 article was later included in the posthumous publication, while the later one was not. In the articles, Muñoz formulates Latino affect as "off," a failing of sorts in relation to affective US whiteness that constructs itself as minimal, underwhelming, and unmarked, "revolv[ing] around an understanding of the Latina/o as affective excess."[1] For Muñoz, the myriad social differences and complexities within Latinidad might be more generatively accounted for through the articulation of a racialized brownness, a "feeling like a problem, in commonality," that enables a better sense of common struggle against hegemonic forces.[2] Brownness, Muñoz suggests, conceptualized as a diversity of affective and performative utterances deriving from Latinonesss, is a potential unifier of Latino people.

The Sense of Brown is a work best understood in the Barthesian fashion of intercalation, "a pure series of interruptions." In his cheekily eponymous *Roland Barthes by Roland Barthes* (1977), the critic describes the German composer Schumann's work as "intercalated," "fragments one after the next."[3] Barthes adapts this approach to his book: fragmented ideas organized according to headings and subheadings with no sense of sequence. The effect is nonlinear, collage-like, and accretive. Knowledge heaps up like a pile of laundry.

The Sense of Brown was compiled in 2020 by editors Joshua Chambers-Letson, a former student of the theorist, and Tavia Nyong'o, Muñoz's friend. Together, they assembled the talks, published articles, and unpublished drafts that the theorist had been saving toward a book-length project on what brownness is, how it operates, and the potential for a brown commons. The editors chose to bookend the work with the most "introduction"- and "conclusion"-like pieces available, since Muñoz himself had yet to write a proper opening and closing, and as a whole the book sidesteps linear argumentation or a comprehensive theory. Like *Disidentifications* and *Cruising Utopia*, *The Sense of Brown* consists of short chapters—intensive case studies largely focused on performance and theater. Most of the performers and playwrights examined are Latina—like Tania Bruguera, María Irene Fornés, and Ana Mendieta—and some are also longtime subjects of Muñoz's work, like Nao Bustamante and Alina Troyano.

The book is significantly shaped by Jean-Luc Nancy's concept of "being singular plural": that being is being-with, that being human is defined by coexistence and plurality. As Nancy puts it: "a mark of union and also a mark of division, a mark of sharing that effaces itself, leaving each term to its isolation *and* its being-with-the-others"[4] always "constitute[d] [by] the traction and tension, repulsion/attraction, of the 'between'-us."[5] Muñoz capaciously conceptualizes brownness as a racialized affect and comportment, as communal feelings situated in the abject and the thrown-away: "feeling brown is feeling together in difference. Feeling brown is an 'apartness together' through the status of being a problem."[6] Throughout the book, Muñoz frequently deploys the term *attunement.* He wants us to pick up on the sensorial nature of brownness—how it can be felt, sensed, and perceived in the here and now. "Owning the negation that is brownness," he writes, "is owning an understanding of self and group as problem in relation to a dominant order, a normative national affect."[7] Although most of the performers he discusses are Latino, and many are Cuban, he explicitly situates brownness against any previously set notion or identity category. He shows how their performances' racialized affect and abject embodiment resist the enclosure of hegemonic neoliberal nationalisms and seek to make legible non-white subjectivities.

Throughout the chapters, in order to better contour what he is getting at, Muñoz points out the differences between his sense of brownness and his earlier theorizing in *Disidentifications* and *Cruising Utopia.* "It is certainly akin to what I described as disidentification," he writes, "but even that description may hinge too much on linearity of direct alignments."[8] And whereas in *Cruising Utopia* he had situated queerness in the not-yet-here of futurity, he locates brownness as "already here," as "vast, present, and vital." As he illustrates with his reading of María Irene Fornés's short play *Mud*, brownness has the paradoxical properties of mud: wetness combined with thick firmness, not quite a liquid and not quite a solid, at once sensuous and discomfiting to the touch. Brownness is shape-shifting, unstable and unpredictable, producing aesthetic responses and embodied affects that are discernable through careful attention. Brownness an attunement to sensing and perceiving the world otherwise.

The Sense of Brown poignantly demonstrates how it is not just the responsibility of the performance or the performer to instantiate what Muñoz calls otherwiseness—"the production and performance of knowledge that does not conform to the mimetic coordinates assigned to both the designations 'wise' and 'other.'"[9] It is also the audience member and the analyst who must co-collaborate brownness into existence through their interpretations. However, this amorphousness of brownness raises questions as to who exactly constitutes and deploys its critical possibilities.

Muñoz emphasizes, and repeatedly reminds us, that brownness is not reducible to Latino identity, and that Latino identity doesn't automatically align with brownness. Latino, he asserts, is not a steady identity that coheres along lines of race, nationality, or language. Rather, it is, citing Norma Alarcón, an "identity-in-difference," or how a group's social difference from the dominant culture is precisely what gives it collective power. Muñoz, following W.E.B. Du Bois's 1903 query in *The Souls of Black Folk*, "How does it feel to be a problem?," postulates that the category of Latino and the possibility for Latinidades is better understood as a problem. We must not sidestep or alleviate the condition of being a problem, but rather dwell in and amplify it. He explains how "brownness is coexistent, affiliates, and intermeshes with blackness, Asianness, indigenousness, and other terms that manifest descriptive force to render the particularities of various modes of striving in the world."[10]

Through the book, Muñoz is at conceptual pains to delimit a more concrete sense of brown that is not reducible to identity, or to a generalized notion of Latino. These reminders are certainly in place to anticipate potential charges of comparativist logic and thinking, to dispel the notion that he is defining brownness as a category equivalent to Blackness, Asianness, and Indigenousness. Yet Muñoz's effort to pin down the Latino category utilized to construct the sense of brown proves difficult, particularly given that many of the performers and sources in the text—such as the non-Black artist Ana Mendieta—are informed by Black aesthetics from Latin America. Scholar Lorgia García-Peña, in her analysis of how Dominican peoples have disassociated from Blackness due to white supremacist ideologies, and how contemporary Latinx identity formation in the United States actively defines itself as not Black, notes how "the common practice of referring to Latino/a/xs as a race—rather than as an arbitrary conglomerate of ethnic and racially diverse peoples who trace their origins to Latin America—further erases Black

Latinxs from literally every space, institution, and possibility of representation."[11] García-Peña's call here is critically important in addressing the rhetorical distinctions that non-Black Latinx people make in distancing themselves from Blackness, in hopes of carving out a kind of raced category distinct from it in the United States. An unspecific, pseudo-universal racialization of the Latinx category cannot be viable if we want to ensure that anti-Blackness comes to its much-needed end.

In 2020, I received an early review copy of *The Sense of Brown* from Duke University Press. I read it while quarantined in my cramped apartment, no vaccine yet. Outside, my fellow New Yorkers were dying en masse. Ambulance sirens rang out at all hours of the day. I double-masked everywhere I went, fearful, bleaching down grocery bags because we weren't yet sure if the virus could spread through surfaces. Death was everywhere, in the air itself. And so I read *The Sense of Brown* unable to stop thinking of death. Mine, potentially my friends' and families', Muñoz's. This posthumous book was quite literally defined by death in all ways imaginable.

After my review published, I was struck by how many people on social media—academics and lay readers alike—were reading the book, or were planning to. It was on most-anticipated reading lists with other trade nonfiction titles. In hopes of landing a wider audience, the book was being identified as an essay collection, not a scholarly monograph. I thought back to the poster of Muñoz at the Queer Liberation March, how he'd been there next to Foucault, Rivera, Johnson, Marx, and all those other queer icons. People were reading him, idolizing him. His words and ideas were circulating. He was roaming the world in ways that indicated, as he himself had once put it, "we cannot anticipate what comes next. The project of theorizing the queer social text is, by its very nature, unfinished."[12] He was no longer my unique obsession.

Had Muñoz . . . made it?

The professor teaching the course I'd taken in 2014 was a friend of Muñoz's. From undergrad to graduate school, I seem to have repeatedly found myself in the orbit of his students and colleagues. All potential ways to him.

2. BROWN MOST HOLY AND HIGH

The first truck my father ever owned, a used Ford pickup, was several shades of brown. The base color was chestnut, with accents of beige and dark brown. It often broke down. Purchased a few years after he'd emigrated from Mexico to the United States, a few years after I was born, he drove it each day to the fields where he worked and returned each evening with the truck thickly coated in dust. When it rained, the unpaved dirt roads in our neighborhood threw their slosh up onto the underside of the truck, caking it in mud. The truck radiated brown, every shade and texture of it, a lumbering, glaring clunker of brownness.

I felt embarrassed when he would drop me off or pick me up from school. The white kids' parents drove small, new, modern cars. Cars that were clean on the outside, free of dust and mud. The white kids' parents didn't work in the fields. They were the landowners and bosses who hired undocumented fieldworkers like my father. These kids and their parents made it known that anyone who worked in the brown of the fields—anyone who was brown—was less than them. My father and I had nothing in common with these people besides our zip code.

Brown, in my childhood imaginary, meant poor, immigrant, dirty, non-white.

Brown meant shame.

Very soon I will have lived more of my life in the city than in the rural farmlands I grew up in. Cities don't offer much in the way of brown. Lots of red brick, lots of silver steel. Most of the brown I see these days is in the brownstones I pass by on the street, which I could never afford. The dogshit on the sidewalk.

I desired, for so long, belonging to what was not brown. Brown meant not normal, not the norm. Berlant summarizes the feeling for me precisely: "To desire belonging to the normal world, the world as it appears, is at root a fantasy of a sense of continuity, a sense of being generally okay; it is a desire to be in proximity to okayness, without passing some test to prove it."[13]

My father cherished his brown Ford pickup. It was his. One thing he could lay claim to on this planet, and he held onto it for at least fifteen years. Until it couldn't run anymore. He replaced it with another used pickup truck, this time a white one. It broke down constantly like its predecessor.

When I think of my father, I think of his brown Ford pickup. Of him driving it down the dirt road to our house in the evenings, his muscular, brown body perched in the front seat, arms extended, steering the wheel. A day's work complete.

"Feeling brown is an 'apartness together' through sharing the status of being a problem," wrote Muñoz.[14] Growing up, I knew my father and I were a problem. Too Mexican, too not-white, too poor, too brown. The other Mexican and Central American folks were thought of in the same way—as a glaring problem in the rural, middle-class white community we called home. A problem that required continual policing, disciplining, and terrorizing. And violence, at times. Our neighborhood was constantly visited by cops and immigration police. We knew ourselves to be a problem. A problem for the white townsfolk, a problem for the local police, a problem for the nation-state itself. We were *their* problem: the problem so needed to confirm who they were, who they weren't, and who they wanted to be. We tried to hide ourselves from view, not take up space, let them walk all over us. This was what was expected. We didn't talk about the problem that we knew ourselves to be. Silence kept us in line.

I never discussed this sense of being a problem with my father until I became an adult. Until I had lived away from my hometown for more than a decade. Because he still lived there, I was careful about how I framed the discussion. I didn't want to hurt him. Make him feel awful about the place he called home. He is a private man, withdrawn. I described to him the rampant racism I had endured at school. The hatred that the town had fomented in me, that I had internalized, of being Mexican, of having a brown father. Some stories of what I went through, enough that he got the point. I told him how depressed I'd been all through my childhood, because of what those people had said and done. He nodded, understanding. Knowing. Sadness lined his face. His deep brown eyes glossy. An inexplicable innocence to his countenance—almost, I think, a pureness. He has had it since I was little, and it has only become more pronounced over time. My father, meek looking, childlike, in the face of my stories.

He took a breath, then recounted some of his own experiences. How employers had robbed him of wages. What people had said to him. He discussed the nature of white people. Why they do what they do, why they live fearfully as they do. We didn't agree on all of it. He acknowledges that racism exists but believes strongly that it's only a few bad apples. I tell him the whole tree is rotten to the roots. He hopes they can do better, make things different. I hope that too, I said to him, but in the meantime we must call them out, demand change, dream another world. He smiled, nodded. Regardless of our different perspectives, for the first time we were able to connect through being a problem. This problem assigned to us that we now reclaim, mobilize, for a politics unimaginable by those white folks in that town. A politics of honesty, one that refuses the rules and norms handed to us. Being a problem never felt so good.

Brown fields, unsown. Clothes stained by the brown dust of the earth. Brown walls.

Brown: the color of my father's labor.

Brown, the filter through which I apprehend my childhood.

Mixing all the paint colors together on a piece of white paper—forming brown.

I do not ascribe Latinx or Latin American identity to a distinct racial category like brown. I understand the common use of "brown" or "brownness" to signal non-white racialized experience, rather than an ontologically stable racial formation between Black and white. Think, for example, of the phrase "Black and Brown people," oft-said in common parlance to signal Black and non-Black racialized peoples—those who are brown skinned, who are undocumented or temporarily documented within the Global North, who are non-English speaking or multilingual, living in distinct ethnic enclaves or barrios, and so on. As scholar Joshua Javier Guzmán explains, "Brown is not an identity. Brown, along with its nominal form, *brownness*, are also not objects of knowledge in the ways that identity markers such as 'Latina/o' or 'Chicana/o' are in the late twentieth and early twenty-first centuries."[15] If brownness—understood as a positionality between white and Black, as it often is—becomes synonymous with Latinx or Latin American, then it inevitably must eject any iteration of Blackness in order to guarantee its distinctiveness, intelligibility, and legitimacy. It must also keep at arm's length other forms of brownness, like Arab or Asian brownness, that threaten its coherence. Muñoz, in 1997, described this tension over designations: "Latin America and Latino American are terms of connivance. They hold together disparate identity shards—national, racial, ethnic, class, and gender components—that refuse to cohere in any 'organic' fashion."[16]

If brown is to mean something for Latinx identity, such a brownness ought to be a staunch commitment to a politics against: against white supremacy, anti-Blackness, settler colonialism, ethnic cleansing, capitalist extraction and destruction, imperialisms old and new.

Brownness less as an identity and more as a set of principles and actions undertaken in pursuit of another world. The politics of brownness as dedicating oneself to a constant learning about where and when and how those –isms occur. Brown as the continued search for revolutionary teachings and ways to implement such revolutions into the everyday. Brown the collaborating on behalf of a freedom not yet realized though imminently possible. Brownness a shared idea of liberation we all have in common.

3. OUR DIVINE TOGETHERNESS

Subsequent Queer Liberation Marches bring more posters of Muñoz. Portraits of him, saint-like. Our deity of queer theory.

More devotees out there than I had realized.

I have only been to the New York City Pride march twice. Once in 2011, when I first arrived in the city as an overeager eighteen-year-old queer, then again as a college senior in 2014. The first time felt like more than enough to get it out of my system, but I went the second time to confirm that I was really over it. I was. I was over the out-of-towners acting rude. The army of cops. The sanitized orderliness of the marching. The many, many corporations there to salute our queerness, to twirl and prance with us in their branded rainbow shirts and lanyards, while behind closed doors they funded anti-LGBTQ politicians and policies. They wanted our dollars but couldn't care less about how the world treats us. These corporations want us to feel represented while shaking our ass on one of their sponsored floats, or while passing by their rainbow-decaled storefronts in June, but when things get tough, when we actually need them to show up for us, they don't. Rainbow capitalism at its finest.

The next Pride march I attended was in 2017, in Mexico City. Queers of all ages and types thronged the streets. There was more mayhem, fewer cops, less corporateness. More my style. Still, I realized yet again, all that distance from New York, that Pride marches aren't for me. Maybe the biggest failing of Pride marches in the twenty-first century is the lack of protest in them. They feel defanged—no bark, no bite. They have no room for concentrated rage at the anti-queer state, no righteous critique of capitalism's ilk. The only acceptable affect is uncritical, unradical bliss. But queers don't get liberated by being nice.

In 2015, trans Latina organizer, activist, and overall badass Jennicet Gutiérrez heckled Barack Obama at a Pride reception event at the White House. Obama was pontificating about his continued hope that LGBTQ people would attain full civil rights. It was a speech that now—on the heels of Trump's presidency, in which he fanned the flames of white supremacy, anti-queerness, and transphobia, revealing all the hatred stewing in the US population and bulldozing the facade of neoliberal feel-goodism that Obama had built a career on—appears cynical and fraught. Gutiérrez shouted for Obama to end all detentions and deportations of LGBTQ immigrants. Obama responded, "You're in my house," to overwhelming applause. What most rattled me about the whole scene when I viewed it online was the way that the crowd jeered at Gutiérrez, shushed her aggressively for speaking up on behalf of a group that rarely gets attention in the public sphere. I could hear a resounding lisp in the shushes and knew that it was other queers—more than likely white gay men—who were so forcefully telling Gutiérrez to shut up.

The shushing haunted me. The hostile response from Obama hadn't been surprising. He was part of the political establishment that favors lip service and pandering over actual care for people's well-being. But my fellow queers? I was caught off guard by the torrent of voices that were not on Gutiérrez's side. These queers wanted nothing to do with queer and trans immigrants. They didn't want to know about how queer life intersects with the militarized border and the booming business of detention centers. They didn't want to hear about the plights of non-white queers. They wanted respectability, inclusion and tolerance, a seat at the imperial table.

In the aftermath, social media only confirmed how many other queers out there felt the same way: Their posts condemned Gutiérrez, mocked her powerful dissent, praised Obama's distasteful retort, became one with the audience that had shushed her. And, simultaneously, they were celebrating the Stonewall riots, the bricks in windows and the queers who'd fought back against cops, Sylvia Rivera and her electrifying indictments against the complicity of white cisgays. As long as queer resistance stayed strictly within the confines of history, they seemed to be saying, then it was okay. But disruption in the here and now was unacceptable.

The shushing resounded the disconnect between us. Those shushing were not my people. Gutiérrez was my people. What she stood for, what she'd done. Heckled, protested, demanded, fought back. This was my Pride.

I try to explain to my boyfriend what Muñoz, this man I never met, means to me. How he inspired me, gave me hope, a language to understand myself and my experience. I flip through my copies of his books, loaded with highlights, trying to show—not just tell—my admiration. I read quotes out loud in my best voice, Shakespearizing theory.

"That's great," my boyfriend says.

"That's all you have to say?" I retort, bristling at his nonchalance.

"Well, you told me why you like his work. I think that's amazing how important it is. What more is there to say?"

I can't make Muñoz mean anything to him. Why should he? Still, I'm devastated. These are my impossible demands. My need for an understanding of my little devotions. For this practice of proximity to the theorist to be recognized.

In a 2013 collection of manifestos on queer media published in *GLQ: A Journal of Lesbian and Gay Studies*, there is a missive by Muñoz expostulating on behalf of a "methexic queer media," one that includes "a call for participation, vivification, and an expanded sense of a queer commons that is not quite present but altogether attainable."[17] The aesthetic term *methexis* is derived from Greek tragedy and refers to the way in which an audience participates in the drama, a kind of group sharing. Muñoz appends onto the queer methetic analytic the language of queer utopianism, the not-yet-here of queerness on the horizon, proffered in the canonical text, *Cruising Utopia*. He will also invoke methexis in *The Sense of Brown*. To instantiate a brown commons, he asserts, brownness is "predicated on a certain mode of methexis,"[18] one that, "permits us to think about how some people's sense of brownness may potentially touch other people's sense of brownness. Brownness is not so much a singular understanding of self as fundamentally additive, knowing that singularities are always part of vaster pluralities."[19] In chapter 12, "The Sense of Wildness," Muñoz, commenting on the work of filmmaker and performer Wu Tsang, yokes together the theoretical ties between *Cruising Utopia* and *The Sense of Brown* through methexis. Tsang's work, he writes, serves as a "touchstone for me in thinking about contemporary art practice that follows a queer methexis, which is one important path to what I am calling a brown commons."[20] Methexis here connects queerness and brownness, second book with final book, a genealogy of thought.

These instantiations of methexis highlight how Muñoz's thinking on the concept was preliminary. His writing on the concept is brief. He clearly wanted to elaborate further upon the term in relation to his theories on brownness, but he didn't have enough time to finish. He had more work to do. His invocation of methexis in both a queer and non-white idiom attended to the ways in which many readers, according to the editors of *The Sense of Brown*, have "appropriate(ed) the pastier passages and ideas from *Cruising Utopia*, whitewashing it by excluding, subordinating, or simply ignoring the analytics of race and racialization that have always been central to Muñoz's work."[21]

As with other works of Muñoz's, *The Sense of Brown* bears the influence of Jean-Luc Nancy. The book repeatedly references sense, which was of particular interest to Nancy's philosophical corpus:

sensing oneself in relation to the world, perceiving a more porous sense of world, and most particularly an emphasis on touch. One way that Muñoz describes brownness, for instance, is "Comprehension through surface touching, a mode of partial knowing as opposed to mastery and masterful knowing."[22] It is not entirely clear, however, if Muñoz was familiar with Nancy's essay on methexis, which was translated into English in 2007 under the title "The Image: Mimesis and Methexis."

Nancy's essay questions the distinction between mimesis and methexis in the figuring of an image. An image is not just mimesis (that is, a reproduction), he claims, but is also shaped by the desires and pleasures of the audience, an entangling of object and subject. For Nancy, as long as one does not position the image as object, as something distinct from oneself, then desire is possible, as is the potential for methexis.[23] Nancy proposes activating a participatory and engaged relation in the world, a becoming worldly (with the world, being-with the world) through sense and sensing. "Not," he writes, "a hypnotism that would at the same time suspend the world of perception and dream in favor of a dry signifying injunction," but a "becom(ing) a moment of the general motion of the world, myself a moment in the general commerce of the senses, of sentiments, of significances."[24] "It is in fascination that methexis takes place," he clarifies. One must be fascinated, must sense through fascination. Fascinating in this context is better used as a verb, as a doing, a fascination that upends to potentially new relations, new commons. Barthes, like Nancy, also finds fascination as key to being-with the image. In the opening comments to the photos in his autobiographically inflected work, *Roland Barthes by Roland Barthes*, he writes: "pleasure is a matter of fascination."[25] An image is not pure mimesis but methetic: an amalgam of interest, fascination, and pleasure that transforms everyone involved.

The poster of Muñoz at my first Queer Liberation March—sainted, robed in his turtleneck—bobs above the marchers, eyeing us holily, austerely. Was it revelation I felt, looking at him, or something akin to transcendence? An aura surrounded his cardboarded image, carving out a space for all to see him, whether they knew who he was or not. But I didn't know exactly what one is supposed to feel upon seeing a saint. The protocols eluded me, a failed Catholic since childhood. I don't believe I ever had a religious experience before seeing that sign. I'd never searched for one, or needed one. I'd had spiritual ones, maybe: the first time I saw a Broadway musical; the time I climbed the volcano Popocatépetl in Mexico; my first time having good sex; listening to Mariah Carey ballads in a steaming hot shower; jogging down half the island of Manhattan. Like those experiences, this moment with the poster undid me in the best way but was unique in its intensity. Someone else—someone besides me, a queer stranger at a protest march—had been so compelled by *this* theorist that they'd made a poster of him. They felt something similar to what I felt.

I couldn't look away. The theorist as saint. The theorist on Sixth Avenue. The theorist emblazoned on a poster at a protest march. The throbbing pulse of all those other queers, shouting and jiving and demanding, surrounded me as I relished Muñoz's postered saintliness. I was wholly immersed in my experience, but I wasn't alone. I was one among our splendid queer many.

"What is a portrait?" German philosopher Hans-Georg Gadamer asks in a 1988 essay, in which he meditates upon a sculpted bust of Plato and parses what exactly makes a portrait a portrait. As he searches for an answer, he philosophizes on mimesis and methexis. The portrait, Gadamer contends, is not merely mimesis or reproduction but is rather an interplay and participatory process. Gadamer takes into account the individual represented in the portrait, and the exertion of individuality that the individual precipitates. According to Gadamer, when we speak of the individual and individuality, it always eludes us: we cannot precisely or legibly demarcate what constitutes the totality of an individual or one's individuality. He asserts that to comprehend an individual is to have "a certain recognition of ourselves," where the individual or portrait is a "playing together of many unique features that brings to life what is fixed."[26] The portrait, as emblematic of the individual, is in Gadamer's formulation only fully intelligible as these muddied and dynamic entanglements between portrait, portraitist, and audience.

Gadamer makes clear that methexis is not just a simple schema of the various parts that comprise a whole. Paraphrasing Plato's dialogue *Parmenides*, in which Socrates urges Zeno to think of the participation of ideas with other ideas rather than participation of the individual with the idea, Gadamer writes that methexis—and, by extension, participation—are best thought of as "like the daylight, distributed over everything, yet without light being separated from light and day being separated from day."[27] The metaphor conveys the importance of coextensiveness: making what we might call daylight requires both the concept of day (knowing that there is a day and night) and material rays of sunlight (that the sun produces beams of light during the day). Both unique on their own terms, but they come together to make what is called "daylight." This rumination on methexis leads Gadamer to further his conclusions on the portrait. The portrait is of an individual, created by an individual. There is a plurality organizing the field of the portrait, where traits of the subject are selected and emphasized for the portrait, and, in turn, the portraitist depicts those traits according to his own style. This, then, creates not a reproduction but a methetic process that "invites us to recognize [the portrait], even when we have seen neither the one represented nor reproductions of him." Gadamer's methexis does not reduce aesthetic production and response to a portrait-portraitist-audience triad whose elements remain fixed and untouching. Rather, Gadamer proposes a methetic evocation and elicitation, where what seems singularly constituted, stable, and mimetic—like a portrait, like the sculpted bust of Plato—is, in fact, a complex and transmogrifying scene, shaped by desires, affects, and histories that are both coordinated and uncoordinated.

Tracing Nancy's and Gadamer's developments upon Plato's methexis brings into relief how Muñoz conceptualizes it in a queerly non-white idiom. Muñoz goes further than the two philosophers in operationalizing methexis for political use, and he does so by grounding his methetic apparatus in the particular that is queer of color performance. In line with his early thinking in *Disidentifications*, he critiques the normatively white mainstream queer media and the limited politics of shows like *Will and Grace*, insisting on the "imperative to think beyond the simply representational and instead imagine a queer media that is methetic in nature."[28] We need new queer realities, he urges, ones not tethered to neoliberal white gay normativities. Queer media, for Muñoz, must be participatory, lively, and plural, engaging with a diversified commons. "The lulling sound of the laugh track," he implores, must be "put aside so we can engage in the production of a vitally methetic queer media that is equally turbulent and productive."[29] And where Nancy argues against "hypnotism," Muñoz similarly asserts that we must not mobilize or imagine based on a deadening relation to performance and media.

Activating a brown commons, according to Muñoz, requires methexis, that "moment in which partition between the performance and the audience lifts or frays and a kind of commons comes into view that is not made by the performance."[30] The intentionality of the performance, and the performance itself, are not as consequential as what happens in between the performance and audience—the commons that emerges in the interstices. How precisely are all the parties involved made into a commons? He provides the example of the footage of Sylvia Rivera's Washington Square Park speech on June 24, 1973, which has by now been widely circulated on social media. Rivera, speaking at the Christopher Street Liberation Day Rally of that year, spoke amid overwhelming boos and jeers on behalf of incarcerated and unhoused queer folks. She forced the predominantly white, cisgender crowd that afternoon to hear her, and to recognize the existence of those at the margins of the queer community. "When you listen to Rivera's words," he writes, "you can hear her demand that the audience think and that they open themselves to the understanding that there is something expansive to the commons, that they, those in attendance, are only a segment of something vaster." He continues, "The audience seems to be with Sylvia as she growls the letters that spell out gay power. Certainly those that are with her have drowned out the voices asking her to shut up. But they are only allowed this moment of methexis, this moment of group sharing and belonging, after they have thought of the commons that includes those beyond a proximate presence."[31]

Rivera's performance allows a methetic opening to occur, one that is—like her—trans, queer, and brown amid the overwhelmingly white, gay, cisgender audience. Muñoz writes that this methetic moment enveloped the audience in front of her but also goes "beyond a proximate presence." Temporally, her methetic performance goes beyond that day in 1973, too. Her voice moves through us in the here and now, half a century later, and moves us to action. We are beyond the moment of the 1973 performance: the beyond that is the fraying, transmogrifying, and mattering across time, space, and self. Here is where Muñoz configures the brown commons as emerging, as more than just the moment of the performance. Here is where methexis generates a political commons and imaginary in opposition to stifling normativities, cruel state-sanctioned violences, and the disposability of queer and non-white bodies.

Rivera's performance and Muñoz's writing of it frays the distinction between performance, critic of performance, and audience. Each informs and transforms the other, multiplying their impacts. The 1973 performance event impacts the various demographics in the audience that day, later becoming meaningful to Muñoz's researching and writing, and effectively expanding the audience to include the reader of today, yesterday, and tomorrow. Many scales are in play, and their multiplicity, plurality, and overall messy entanglements are significant for a queer of color methetic method. This triadic messiness between Rivera, Muñoz, and the audience(s) recall Muñoz's reading of the Fornés's play *Mud*, in which he notes the play's "exhilarating" "connection between brownness and mud." The connection is mainly symbolic: the characters feel stuck in the mud and want something better. Muñoz, however, shows how Mae, the protagonist, wants the good life that is metaphorically linked to whiteness, therefore foreclosing her from "sync[ing] with the brownness of a vaster brown commons."[32]

Methexis as queer of color method exemplifies these qualities of mud: shape-shifting, unstable and unpredictable, producing aesthetic tactics and responses that are discernable through careful attention. The interplay of Rivera and Muñoz is about attunement to the world otherwise. It is about this being-with with one another through performing, researching, and writing; this uncertain zone of what-ifs and what-nexts, where many dally on the daily; feelings and comportments and practices unbecoming, in many ways like mud, muddying up the structures and powers and protocols that seek to purify, standardize, and do away with the many weirdos, queens, and down-and-outs, these plenty who imagine elsewhere for who we can be, what we can know, and how we can study otherwise.

4. HANGING OUT WITH HOPE

I glued white paper onto cardboard, the backdrop. Printed out a picture of him, the black-and-white one where he's younger and in his turtleneck. Baby-faced Muñoz, the theorist just beginning. My favorite photo of him, and one so different from the deified image on the poster I saw at my first Queer Liberation March in 2019. The resolution in the printed picture was, unfortunately, low, but it would be fine. Marchers would either know or not know the face, and besides, all that mattered was that I was contributing my Muñozian tribute to the Queer Liberation March of 2023. I plastered his mug on the white paper. I wasn't sure what other elements to add in order to zhuzh it up. Glitter? Paint? Confetti? I needed a quote of his, too, for impact. Which one? Theorists can be quite wordy, favoring their hypotactic syntax structures, the mystique of the obtuse. All the quotes I liked were too long. Trying to jam them into a poster would be ridiculous. I needed something punchy that the other marchers could take in within seconds.

Lo and behold, nothing came to me. Not to mention there was a certain finesse missing from my poster. It didn't look as good as the Muñoz poster at the first Queer Liberation March. I have never been artistically inclined in such ways, so I don't know what I was expecting. Or what I wanted, exactly. Or what I ever really want, Libra that I am. I put the unfinished poster in my closet and went out to the streets for another march. Muñoz in my closet. My own private ofrenda.

Unlike in *Disidentifications* and *Cruising Utopia*, there are noticeably fewer Muñozian anecdotes in *The Sense of Brown*. Fewer stories about his childhood, fewer descriptions of him attending the performances he would then write on. The case studies are mainly analytical—close readings that dazzle with their perspectives. Muñoz worked on the manuscript that would become *The Sense of Brown* for fifteen years. Fifteen years of drafts kept in a black binder. An incomplete book, unfinished thinking.

Odds are that he would have added the anecdotes later, giving us a sense of the order of his writing process. I wonder where in the existing manuscript would he have inserted himself. At what points in the writing did he see the relevance of his life, his journeys, as pertinent to the theorizing. When would he have shared with us *him*.

A professor once told me that I overshare when analyzing texts. No one cares about the person doing the close reading, they informed me. Act like you're not even there.

Muñoz depositing drafts into the black binder. Some published articles, some unpublished chapters. Muñoz rifling through the pages, pondering the completed manuscript to come, the day he will complete the writing. He safekeeps what he has so far in the binder:

a place to hold ideas, the hope of the future manuscript. I imagine that, throughout his fifteen years of thinking, he returns to the binder regularly, like a beloved friend. Returns again and again to the book he knows not how to finish.

I have never been able to abide by the rule of the disembodied, disinterested critic.

Was he stuck? On what the exact thesis of the book would be? On how to write it out for an audience? Fifteen years is a long time. A long time to be stuck, if that was the case. I wonder if being stuck is also a site of possibility. Where thought can happen, albeit maybe not as productively as one would hope, in a way that is not totally conducive to finishing a book. Maybe he was stuck on thinking, stuck in a loop of ideas, stuck on fixation—might there be something tantalizing about stuckness? To linger, to dwell, to obsess without climax, a constant state of edging toward. If he was stuck on *The Sense of Brown* for all those years, I want to think it was because he was cooking up something grand, altogether unheard of. Getting himself in theoretical knots, needing to unknot a concept that didn't quite work yet. Formulating then reformulating an idea, refusing to settle for a single conclusion.

Fetishizing stuckness as a means of valuing the practice of thinking. Where thought is, in and of itself, worthy of the undertaking.

In a world mired in disinformation, where those in power work to coerce the masses into believing structural oppression and state violence are necessary, thinking becomes a political act. I do not mean here the type of sentiment that finds expression in the sound bites "Think for yourself," or "Be an independent thinker." These oft-stated phrases, widely repeated in countries like the United States and the United Kingdom, traffic in possessive individualism, fantasies of mastery, and dog-eat-dog mentalities, which are precisely the problem at hand. In this context, to think independently is to think in the interest of oneself, detached from history and society, denying our responsibility to cohabit with other humans and the world at large. Our so-called independent thinking forsakes the collective good and mutual flourishing. This framework has allowed greed, self-interest, and the pursuit of power to masquerade as a form of autonomy in which one's agency to think independently above all else comes at great cost: the hubris to do what one wants without having to account for facts, knowledge, or others. None of us can ever, truly, think outside the boxes constituting our lives. None of us can rid ourselves of the contexts, frameworks, and societies that provide the language, the conceptual resources, in which to even articulate ourselves. Being a truly independent thinker is therefore a tantalizing impossibility.

One can be, however, a conscientious thinker. One who pursues thinking in order to unthink the logics handed down, the rationalities spoon-fed to us to limit our capacity to imagine. One can seek to get stuck in thinking, a stuckness that strives to delink from violent systems and repressive structures in order to inaugurate new forms and relations. Thinking that is informed, attuned to histories and contexts, a curiosity of thought that aspires for another kind of world, a different way of knowing what the world can be. Thought as a practice of hope, aligning with, following Ernst Bloch, Muñoz's concept of "educated hope."

"I am making a distinction between a mode of hope that simply keeps one in place within an emotional situation predicated on control," he postulates in a 2009 dialogue with his friend, the scholar Lisa Duggan, "and, instead, a certain practice of hope that helps escape from a script in which human existence is reduced."[33] Here he speaks of politically vacuous hope that we often hear out of politicians, feel-good optimism and compulsory happiness that relies upon inaction, complacency, and the individual over the communal. Hope, in Muñoz's theoretical oeuvre, is part and parcel of his notion of queer utopianism, necessary for enacting another sense of the world: "Practicing educated hope is the enactment of a critique function. It is not about announcing the way things *ought* to be, but, instead imagining what things *could* be. It is thinking beyond the narrative of what stands for the world today by seeing it as not enough."[34]

Thinking as a radical practice that, like educated hope, aspires after that transformative energy residing in the subjunctive. To be able to think up a world that does not yet exist but could, if we work for it.

Maybe he wasn't stuck. Maybe he just didn't have enough time in his schedule to work on the manuscript. Too much teaching to do, too many letters of recommendation to write, too many university committees to run. Overworked. He was running a department, after all, in the last years of his life. Academia, one of the rare jobs where you get paid to research. Academia, where you also can't get any research done.

"Hope's biggest obstacle is failure," Muñoz stated in September 2013, in what would be one of his last public lectures before his death.[35] The lecture, later included in the tenth-anniversary edition of *Cruising Utopia*, was given to honor the opening of the Women and Gender Studies Institute PhD program at the University of Toronto. Like all beginnings, there is hope. One needs hope in order to start something new. Hope, often, feels intimately linked to newness. I find it intriguing that Muñoz so boldly opened his lecture, on the eve of a new academic program, in a space more than likely inundated with hopeful students, faculty, and administrators alike, on how hope fails us. How humans lose hope, too often. But that is the nature of hope, Muñoz stresses, and that is why we must continue returning to it. Even in the face of disappointment, hope must remain. A lesson no more important than in the halls of academe, where the first programs to have their funding cut or be on the receiving end of right-wing attacks are those like women's studies. Disciplines like women's studies are haunted by the specter of failure, by coordinated assaults that are counting on hope to wane, to disappear. Hopelessness is the right-hand man of power. In this case, the persistence of hope is all the more needed, even if in the periphery, unseen though present.

So Muñoz, with his opening remark, is prepping the room for the struggles ahead. For university austerity measures that results in humanities departments being severely defunded or shuttered entirely, the students paying the price. For the continued under-resourcing of doctoral education and the undermining of humanities research in advancing society for the better. For the battle against state-sponsored disinformation and fascist coercion that perpetuates and normalizes structural violence, willful ignorance, and systemic oppression. His speech to that new program was a rallying cry. He needed the room to know that maintaining hope is a challenge, and that the challenge cannot be forsaken. "Hope is a risk. But if the point is to change the world we must risk hope," he urges.[36]

Even as I write this now, I am stuck on this project. Both stuck on thinking about it, and stuck on how to write it. Stuck on how to share with others why the theorist is so important. How to make him matter not just to me but to everyone, in some way. Stuck, probably, because the object of analysis feels too close, yet so far, nowhere really. The relation complicated. Muñoz: "Objects, loved objects, objects of knowledge, objects we hope to form invincible bonds with, disappoint us, but that is all the more reason to understand the nature of the incommensurability that structures our being-with."[37] I am not sure how to say what I want to say. Words come to me, evoking a particular meaning I am unsure about, then I delete. The blank page my enemy. I am always revising, editing what little I have. For the first time in my life I am editing obsessed, am living for it. There are no darlings to kill here. I am afraid of my approach being misunderstood. This *too*-personal writing about a theorist. Not wanting the stuckness to be permanent, all-encompassing as it seems to be, though also knowing keenly that stuckness excites, exhausts, enthralls. I'm stuck on Muñoz, and I don't know if I will get unstuck. Don't know if I want to.

......

Hopelessness occurs. Inching its tendrils into our psyches, those little whispers repeating. "All is lost," "Why keep going?," "Just give up." We feel down, unendurably down, sometimes to the point where the whispers sound about right. Nothing will change. Why bother? Hopelessness happens to all of us, as the queer theorist himself knew, but he instructs us to not forget that "hopelessness need not be the breakdown of politics, but, instead, can be a bad sentiment that, through virtuoso performance, may become newly politically relevant."[38] Hopelessness repurposed, mobilized. Don't let it go to waste. Don't let it waste us. Following a line of thinking set forth by his mentor Sedgwick, he theorized that "the depressive position is a site of potentiality and not simply a breakdown of the self or the social fabric. Reparation is part of the depressive position; it signals a certain kind of hope."[39] We feel down, we feel hopeless, we get in our feelings—but we can make lemonade out of those moldy lemons. The hopeless put back on track for a critical hope.

In the summer of 2013, Muñoz ventured out to the Bronx to visit his friend Fred Moten, who was presenting a poem at the Gramsci Monument, an installation at a public housing complex called the Forest Houses. The plywood-based participatory installation, created by the Swiss artist Thomas Hirschhorn, had been inspired by the Italian Marxist Antonio Gramsci and, across the grounds of the complex, contained a library, newspaper press, computer room, museum, radio station, bar, workshop, classroom, and a theater with white lawn chairs for seating. Residents of the Forest Houses had helped construct the installation, which was now open to all between July 1 and September 15. The installation hosted events ranging from lectures to workshops to music performances to the poetry reading that Muñoz would later reflect on in one of his final writings: "The Event of the Poem: 'the gramsci monument.'"

The short essay was published posthumously, in 2014. In it, Muñoz describes what he saw on that mild summer day: how the installation "looked as though Sun Ra had landed a plywood space station in the middle of the Forest House ground," how he'd found Moten writing the poem in the Gramsci memorial library, how Moten had rhapsodized on the idea of the projects: "let's bust the project up. let's love the project. can the / projects be loved? we love the projects."[40] Moten's poem shoots out variations of the word *project* like fireworks—repetitions as reclamations of what the projects can signify. The poem takes back the city projects for another political project, that the state could not have anticipated: "we violate the auction / block experiment. we pirates of ourselves and others."[41] Muñoz picks up on this thread of piracy—on the reclamation of violent signifiers of state power—and amplifies it. Wood is foundational to the installation itself, he theorizes, and, "could, from a certain perspective, symbolize only chattel slavery's auction block but, in this instance, during the event of the poem, signals the material that allows us to imagine a pirate ship in the projects, holding its passengers and participants who feel held by the hold."[42] K'eguro Macharia echoes this sentiment of not letting violence foreclose horizons in the final pages of his *Frottage*:

> the noose the bullet the lynching the poisoning the bombing the
> camps the mass graves the killing that makes futures difficult
> but not impossible
> never impossible.[43]

Wood resignifies because we can imagine it so. Desiring resignification like desiring love in all its many guises, desiring all the transformations we yearn for love to make upon us, hopeful that, as Berlant explains, our pursuit "continues to exert a utopian promise to discover a form that is elastic enough to manage what living throws at lovers."[44] Malleable materials, repurposed for what comes next. Sedgwick, in her poem "Death," brings another angle: "The point's not what becomes you, but what's you."[45] Not impossible and never impossible, yet elastic enough to manage what living throws at what we are. Revolution demands our many-voiced articulations. "This pirate ship is also a spaceship," Muñoz quips, whose "destination is the necessity of radical departure from one singular project to a vaster sense of a plurality of projects."

Pirate ships into spaceships, free-flying across sea and cosmos, the theorist must have mused, while seated on a white lawn chair listening to his friend's poem in the makeshift theater. Around him, as he daydreamed in his black-framed glasses, the towering brown-bricked edifices of the projects, those agonizingly bland products of New York City's investment in, then divestment from, the poor, must have taken new shape. Brown projects of possibility. Brown rockets readying to launch into the elsewhere of outer space: brown ships taking off into the distant sea: brown submarines torpedoing into the dark vastness: brown structures of the wayward imagination. Poetry resounded across those brown-bricked buildings. Moten's poem, yes. But also the sounds of the project's residents: the children playing and screaming, boom boxes blaring out tunes, grandmothers gossiping, friends or lovers shouting greetings to each other from a block away. All together these city sounds must have clashed, synthesized, in the theorist's reverie. Knowing him, the theorist must have projected that delightful discord into the dream he had dreamed for so long. The dream of disidentifying. The dream of the ephemeral. The dream of the queer utopic. The dream of brownness. The dream that thought and imagination and ideas can transform the present reality. The dream that even the brown-bricked facades of the projects can be a site to unmake, and remake, the world.

He sat in a white lawn chair on that mild summer day in 2013, and dreamed.

We've been chasing after him ever since.

CODA

TÍO JOSÉ

I have no fondness for any of my biological tíos whom I've met. Many of them are emotionally and physically abusive to partners, children, siblings, and strangers alike. Many of them, if not all, are to varying degrees sexist, racist, homophobic, and transphobic, and unapologetically so. I have no relationship with any of them anymore, for these very reasons, and so in a way they don't really live up to the appellation of tío. I feel no affection for them. I am sure they feel the same about me, the flamboyant homosexual of the family. Several of them not only are offended but are also disgusted by my queerness, to the point that they no longer even ask my mother or father how I am doing. So I call them by their first names when I see them and discuss them with others. They do not get to be my Tío Ramón or my Tío Luis. A capital T tío. There is no love in our relations. No bonds that unite us. We merely share some genetics.

The only exception is the tío I never got to meet. My queer tío who lived with and died from HIV/AIDS. My Tío Cano.

He is my tío because his foreshortened queer life helped make it possible for queer people like me to live on after him. The bits and pieces that I know of him have guided, nurtured, and held me, which is what family does. The speculations I have about how he lived and thought compel me, as a good tío does, to live a life that is abundant with joy, compassion, honesty, and a mandate to care for others. I have only ever known my Tío Cano as a ghost. His love has been given to me from a beyond—not just the beyond of death, but also the beyond of never having known his spirit on this mortal realm. Yet I honor this idiosyncratic love no less than any love I've had with the living.

I have loved ghosts of all kinds: a tío never met; a brother known for but twelve short years before he passed away; a grandmother who was a mother; the authors and artists no longer here who still inspire; the dancers and lovers and partyers who perished at Pulse; the many colonized and oppressed who fought for, and dreamed up, other ways of living together in this world. Ghosts can love us as we should be loved when the living do not know how. And we, in return, love them, though we may have never even crossed paths. We practice this love through the commitments we make to the living. To live authentically, to live justly, to live fiercely—some things my Tío Cano taught me.

Another ghost I have never met: José Esteban Muñoz. And, like my tío, I can't help but love him too. For a long time, I felt I had no connection to him. I was never his student, nor his colleague, nor anything to him while he was alive. Yet I have learned through the process of writing this book that I can nonetheless claim Muñoz as someone close to me, as a familiar, a ghost loved. I needed his words in my life. I needed to know that someone like him had lived.

I think that is what love is, really: that needing so indescribably intense—somehow both material and immaterial, real and unreal, its thrall ravenous and consuming, yet always inexplicably divine, singularly yours—that you can't imagine life without it. For that reason, love pushes us to do better, drives us to the brink, changes hearts and minds. Love also hurts and disappoints. Love, sometimes, runs its course. Love propels revolt and revolution. Love breaks us. Love is the creative force behind imagining, and enacting, a different arrangement for this world we share. Love endures.

I have no interest in being anyone's tío. The masculine emphasis of the designation repels me. Maybe Muñoz wouldn't identify in such a way either. Perhaps a queer titi would suit us both best. For now, though, I want to think of the theorist as a tío to me. A capital T Tío. My Tío José.

ACKNOWLEDGMENTS

All my gratitude to Catherine Tung, who made this book what it is. Her feedback, support, and our conversations have been invaluable. To Lauren Abramo, as always, for all that she does. Where would I be without her guidance and care? To the team at Beacon who have helped bring this book into the world—an immense thank you.

My father, Santiago, the first theorist I loved in my life, mil gracias. Es un honor ser tu hijo.

And to those everyday theorists I have learned from throughout the years: the farmworkers, the high school English teachers, the janitors and the housekeepers, the food vendors and the subway singers, and all those many others. Your theories are transforming the world for the better.

NOTES

1: THE THEORY OF FALLING IN LOVE WITH THEORY

1. José Esteban Muñoz, *Disidentifications: Queers of Color and the Performance of Politics* (Minneapolis: University of Minnesota Press, 1999), 160.

2. Muñoz, *Disidentifications,* 30.

3. Jonathan Beller, "Theory Hogs of the Political Unconscious," *Social Text* 32, no. 4 (Winter 2014): 167–77, https://doi.org/10.1215/01642472-2820544.

4. Roderick A. Ferguson, *Aberrations in Black: Toward A Queer of Color Critique* (Minneapolis: University of Minnesota Press, 2003), 24.

5. K'eguro Macharia, "On Being Area-Studied: A Litany of Complaint," *GLQ* 22, no. 2 (April 2016): 183–89, https://doi.org/10.1215/10642684-3428711.

6. Phillip Brian Harper, Anne McClintock, José Esteban Muñoz, and Trish Rosen, "Queer Transexions of Race, Nation, and Gender: An Introduction," *Social Text,* nos. 52/53 (1997): 1–4, http://www.jstor.org/stable/466731.

7. José Esteban Muñoz, "Queer Minstrels for the Straight Eye: Race as Surplus in Gay TV," *GLQ* 11, no. 1 (January 2005): 101–2, https://doi.org/10.1215/10642684-11-1-101.

8. José Esteban Muñoz, "Dead White: Notes on the Whiteness of the New Queer Cinema," *GLQ* 4, no. 1 (January 2005): 127–38, https://doi.org/10.1215/10642684-4-1-127.

9. José Esteban Muñoz and John Vincent, "My Own Private Latin America: Notes on the Trade in Latino Bodies," *Dispositio/n* 23, no. 50 (1998/2000): 19–36.

10. Muñoz and Vincent, "My Own Private Latin America," 21.

11. David L. Eng, Judith Halberstam, and José Esteban Muñoz, "Introduction: What's Queer About Queer Studies Now?" *Social Text* 23, nos. 3–4 (2005): 1–17, https://doi.org/10.1215/01642472-23-3-4_84-85-1.

12. Muñoz, *Disidentifications*, 4.

13. Eve Kosofsky Sedgwick, *Tendencies* (Durham, NC: Duke University Press, 1993), 264.

14. Muñoz, *Disidentifications*, xv.

15. "Munoz, Jose Esteban," obituary, *New York Times*, December 10, 2013, https://archive.nytimes.com/query.nytimes.com/gst/fullpage-9800E7D81E3AF933A25751C1A9659D8B63.html.

16. Roland Barthes, *Mourning Diary*, trans. Richard Howard (New York: Hill and Wang, 2010), 73.

17. José Esteban Muñoz, *Cruising Utopia* (New York: New York University Press, 2009), xxi.

18. Roland Barthes, *Camera Lucida*, trans. Richard Howard (New York: Hill and Wang, 2010), 67.

19. Barthes, *Camera Lucida*, 71.

20. Barthes, *Camera Lucida*, 72.

21. Eve Kosofsky Sedgwick, *Touching Feeling: Affect, Pedagogy, Performativity* (Durham, NC: Duke University Press, 2003), 2.

22. Eve Kosofsky Sedgwick, *Between Men: English Literature and Male Homosocial Desire* (1985; New York: Columbia University Press, 2015), xix.

23. bell hooks, "Theory as Liberatory Practice," *Yale Journal of Law and Feminism* 4, no. 1 (Fall 1991): 1–12.

24. José Esteban Muñoz, "Teaching, Minoritarian Knowledge, and Love," *Women & Performance: a journal of feminist theory* 14, no. 2 (June 2008): 117–21, https://doi.org/10.1080/07407700508571480.

25. Muñoz, "Teaching, Minoritarian Knowledge, and Love," 120.

26. Muñoz, "Teaching, Minoritarian Knowledge, and Love," 121.

27. Jordan Stein, *Avidly Reads Theory* (New York: New York University Press, 2019), 54.

28. Eve Kosofsky Sedgwick, "Paranoid Reading and Reparative Reading; or, You're So Paranoid, You Probably Think This Introduction Is About You," in *Novel Gazing: Queer Readings in Fiction*, ed. Eve Kosofsky Sedgwick (Durham, NC: Duke University Press, 1997), 23.

29. Sedgwick, *Tendencies*, 1.

30. José Esteban Muñoz, "Famous and Dandy Like B. 'n' Andy: Race, Pop, and Basquiat," in *Pop Out: Queer Warhol*, ed. Jennifer Doyle, Jonathan Flatley, and José Esteban Muñoz (Durham, NC: Duke University Press, 1996), 144.

31. Juana María Rodríguez, *Sexual Futures, Queer Gestures, and Other Latina Longings* (New York: New York University, 2014), 35.

32. Eve Kosofsky Sedgwick, "Queer and Now," in *Wild Orchids and Trotsky: Messages from American Universities*, ed. Mark Edmundson (New York: Penguin, 1993), 239.

33. Judith Butler, "Solidarity/Susceptibility," *Social Text* 36, no. 4 (2018): 1–20, https://doi.org/10.1215/01642472-7145633.

34. Butler, "Solidarity/Susceptibility," 2.

35. Lee Edelman, "On Solidarity," *Representations* 158, no. 1 (2022): 93–105, https://doi.org/10.1525/rep.2022.158.10.93.

36. Edelman, "On Solidarity," 94.

37. Edelman, "On Solidarity," 105.

38. José Esteban Muñoz, "The Heteroglossia of Queer Voices," *LGSN: Lesbian and Gay Studies Newsletter* (July 1992): 35–36.

39. José Esteban Muñoz, "The Wildness of the Punk Rock Commons," *South Atlantic Quarterly* 117, no. 3 (July 2018): 453–64, https://doi.org/10.1215/00382876-6942219.

40. Judith Butler, *Gender Trouble: Feminism and the Subversion of Identity* (New York: Routledge, 1990), xix.

41. Jack Halberstam and Tavia Nyong'o, "Introduction: Theory in the Wild," *South Atlantic Quarterly* 117, no. 3 (July 2018): 653–58, https://doi.org/10.1215/00382876-6942081.

42. Eve Kosofsky Sedgwick and Adam Frank, "Shame in the Cybernetic Fold: Reading Silvan Tomkins," in *Shame and Its Sisters: A Silvan Tomkins Reader*, ed. Eve Kosofsky Sedgwick and Adam Frank (Durham, NC: Duke University Press, 1995), 23.

43. K'eguro Macharia, *Frottage: Frictions of Intimacy Across the Black Diaspora* (New York: New York University Press, 2019), 126.

44. Lauren Berlant, *Cruel Optimism* (Durham, NC: Duke University Press, 2011), 2.

45. Roland Barthes, *How to Live Together: Novelistic Simulations of Some Everyday Spaces*, trans. Kate Briggs (New York: Columbia University Press, 2012), 127.

46. José Esteban Muñoz, "Chicana Writing: Fiction," in *The Oxford Companion to Women's Writing in the United States*, ed. Cathy N. Davidson, Linda Wagner-Martin, Elizabeth Ammons, Trudier Harris, Ann Kibbey, Amy Ling, and Janice Radway (New York: Oxford University Press, 1995), 171.

II: HE HAD TO HAVE . . .

1. José Esteban Muñoz, "Ephemera as Evidence: Introductory Notes to Queer Acts," *Women & Performance: a journal of feminist theory* 8, no. 2 (1996): 5–16, https://doi.org/10.1080/07407709608571228.

2. Eve Kosofsky Sedgwick, "Queer Performativity: Henry James's *The Art of the Novel*," *GLQ: Gay and Lesbian Quarterly* 1, no. 1 (1993): 1–16, https://doi.org/10.1215/10642684-1-1-1.

3. José Esteban Muñoz, *Cruising Utopia: The Then and There of Queer Futurity* (New York: New York University Press, 2009), 65.

4. Fred Moten, *B Jenkins* (Durham, NC: Duke University Press, 2010), 39.

5. Mary Ann Doane, *Bigger Than Life: The Close-Up and Scale in the Cinema* (Durham, NC: Duke University Press, 2022), 38.

6. Doane, *Bigger Than Life*, 49.

7. Doane, *Bigger Than Life*, 35.

8. José Esteban Muñoz, *The Sense of Brown* (Durham, NC: Duke University Press, 2020), 139.

9. Lauren Berlant and Lee Edelman, *Sex, or the Unbearable* (Durham, NC: Duke University Press, 2013), 125.

10. Joshua Lubin-Levy and Ricardo Montez, "Curatorial Statement," *Ephemera as Evidence*, 9.

11. Jean-Luc Nancy, "Ode to José Esteban Muñoz," trans. Damon R. Young, *Social Text 32*, no. 4 (Winter 2014): 9–12, https://doi.org/10.1215/01642472-2820412.

12. Muñoz, "Ephemera as Evidence," 6.

13. José Esteban Muñoz, "Reviewed Work(s): Uncloseting Drama: American Modernism and Queer Performance by Nick Salvato," *Theatre Journal* 64, no. 4 (December 2012): 618–19.

III: IN THE OFFICE WITH YOU

1. Diana Taylor, "What Is Performance Studies?" interview with José Muñoz, Hemispheric Institute of Performance and Politics, New York University, 2002, https://sites.dlib.nyu.edu/hidvl/m63xsjsw.

2. José Esteban Muñoz, *Cruising Utopia: The Then and There of Queer Futurity* (New York: New York University Press, 2009), 1.

3. Robert L. Caserio, Lee Edelman, Judith Halberstam, José Esteban Muñoz, and Tim Dean, "Forum: Conference Debates: The Antisocial Thesis in Queer Theory," *PMLA* 121, no. 3 (May 2006): 819–28, https://www.jstor.org/stable/25486357.

4. Caserio, Edelman, Halberstam, Muñoz, and Dean, "Forum: Conference Debates: The Antisocial Thesis in Queer Theory," 826.

5. Muñoz, *Cruising Utopia, 28.*

6. Muñoz, "Ephemera as Evidence," 14.

7. José Esteban Muñoz, *Disidentifications: Queers of Color and the Performance of Politics* (Minneapolis: University of Minnesota Press, 1999), 25.

8. José Esteban Muñoz, "A Forum on Theatre and Tragedy: A Response to September 11," *Theatre Journal* 54, no. 1 (March 2002): 123.

9. "Cruising Utopia: The Then and There of Queer Futurity," by José Esteban Muñoz, review, *Publishers Weekly*, September 28, 2009, https://www.publishersweekly.com/9780814757284.

10. Oscar Wilde, *De Profundis* (1905; New York: Penguin, 2000), 110.

11. D. A. Miller, *Bringing Out Roland Barthes* (Oakland: University of California Press, 1992), 6.

12. José Esteban Muñoz, *Cruising Utopia: The Then and There of Queer Futurity, 10th-Anniversary Edition* (New York: New York University Press, 2019), 207.

13. Ernst Bloch, *The Utopian Function of Art and Literature: Selected Essays*, trans. Jack Zipes and Frank Mecklenburg (Cambridge, MA: MIT Press, 1988), 243–44.

14. Muñoz, *Cruising Utopia*, 166.

15. Ramón H. Rivera-Servera, *Performing Queer Latinidad: Dance, Sexuality, Politics* (Ann Arbor: University of Michigan Press, 2012), 34.

16. Muñoz, *Cruising Utopia*, 68.

17. Eve Kosofsky Sedgwick, *Tendencies* (Durham, NC: Duke University Press, 1993), 157.

18. Muñoz, *Cruising Utopia*, 68.

19. Muñoz, *Cruising Utopia*, 69.

20. Muñoz, *Cruising Utopia*, 69.

21. Miller, *Bringing Out Roland Barthes*, 39.

IV: SUIT JACKET INFORMALITIES

1. Eve Kosofsky Sedgwick, *Tendencies* (Durham, NC: Duke University Press, 1993), 113.

2. Wayne Koestenbaum, "Foreword," in Eve Kosofsky Sedgwick, *Between Men: English Literature and Male Homosocial Desire* (1985; New York: Columbia University Press, 2015), xvi.

3. Sedgwick, *Tendencies*, 155.

4. Sedgwick, *Tendencies*, 164.

5. Wayne Koestenbaum, *My 1980s & Other Essays* (New York: FSG Originals, 2013), 66.

6. Eve Kosofsky Sedgwick, "Queer Performativity: Warhol's Shyness/Warhol's Whiteness," in *Pop Out: Queer Warhol*, ed. Jennifer Doyle, Jonathan Flatley, and José Esteban Muñoz (Durham, NC: Duke University Press, 1996), 132.

7. Lauren Berlant, "Reading Sedgwick, Then and Now," in *Reading Sedgwick*, ed. Lauren Berlant (Durham, NC: Duke University Press, 2019), 2.

8. Jacques Derrida, *The Post Card: From Socrates to Freud and Beyond*, trans. Allan Bass (Chicago: University of Chicago Press, 1987), 11.

9. Ellison Hanson, "The Future's Eve: Reparative Reading After Sedgwick," *South Atlantic Quarterly* 110, no. 1 (January 2011): 101–19, https://doi.org/10.1215/00382876-2010-025.

10. Gary Fisher, *Gary in Your Pocket: Stories and Notebooks of Gary Fisher*, ed. Eve Kosofsky Sedgwick (Durham, NC: Duke University Press, 1996), 208.

11. Fisher, *Gary in Your Pocket*, 185.

12. José Esteban Muñoz, *Cruising Utopia: The Then and There of Queer Futurity, 10th-Anniversary Edition* (New York: New York University Press, 2019), 194.

13. Muñoz, *Cruising Utopia, 10th-Anniversary Edition*, 199.

14. Fisher, *Gary in Your Pocket*, 180.

15. Eve Kosofsky Sedgwick, *A Dialogue on Love* (Boston: Beacon Press, 2000), 160–61.

16. Eve Kosofsky Sedgwick, *Fat Art, Thin Art* (Durham, NC: Duke University Press, 1994), 13.

17. Kosofsky Sedgwick, *Fat Art, Thin Art*, 14.

18. K'eguro Macharia, "Queer Writing, Queer Politics: Working Across Difference," in *The Cambridge Companion to Queer Studies*, ed. Siobhan B. Somerville (Cambridge: Cambridge University Press, 2020), 41.

19. Assotto Saint, *Spells of a Voodoo Doll* (New York: Richard Kasak Book, 1996), 89.

20. Sedgwick, *A Dialogue on Love*, 127.

21. Fisher, *Gary in Your Pocket*, 213.

22. Fisher, *Gary in Your Pocket*, 276.

23. Sedgwick, *A Dialogue on Love*, 179.

24. Fisher, *Gary in Your Pocket*, 291.

25. Eve Kosofsky Sedgwick, *Epistemology of the Closet* (Oakland: University of California Press, 1990), 25.

26. Fisher, *Gary in Your Pocket*, 259.

27. Sedgwick, *A Dialogue on Love*, 213.

28. Lauren Berlant, *Cruel Optimism* (Durham, NC: Duke University Press, 2011), 1.

29. Berlant, *Cruel Optimism*, 24.

30. José Esteban Muñoz, "Citizens and Superheroes," *American Quarterly* 52, no. 2 (June 2000): 397–404.

31. Lauren Berlant, "Eve Sedgwick, Once More," *Critical Inquiry* 35, no. 4 (Summer 2009): 1089–91, https://doi.org/10.1086/605402.

32. Lauren Berlant, *On the Inconvenience of Other People* (Durham, NC: Duke University Press, 2022), 74.

33. José Esteban Muñoz, *Disidentifications: Queers of Color and the Performance of Politics* (Minneapolis: University of Minnesota Press, 1999), 99.

34. José Esteban Muñoz, "Letters to the Editor: Window-Dressing?" *American Theatre* (September 2004): 3.

35. José Esteban Muñoz, "The Sense of Watching Tony Sleep," in *After Sex? On Writing Since Queer Theory*, ed. Janet Halley and Andrew Parker (Durham, NC: Duke University Press, 2011), 142.

36. Muñoz, "The Sense of Watching Tony Sleep," 149.

37. Lauren Berlant with Jay Prosser, "Life Writing and Intimate Publics: A Conversation with Lauren Berlant," *Biography* 34, no. 1 (Winter 2011): 180–87, https://www.jstor.org/stable/23541186.

38. Lauren Berlant, *The Queen of America Goes to Washington City: Essays on Sex and Citizenship* (Durham, NC: Duke University Press, 1997), 265.

39. José Esteban Muñoz, "Rough Boy Trade: Queer Desire/Straight Identity in the Photography of Larry Clark," in *The Passionate Camera: Photography and Bodies of Desire*, ed. Deborah Bright (New York: Routledge, 1998), 167.

40. Muñoz, "Rough Boy Trade," 167.

V: TURN THE PULSE AROUND

1. José Esteban Muñoz, *The Sense of Brown* (Durham, NC: Duke University Press, 2020), 141.

2. José Esteban Muñoz, "A Forum on Theatre and Tragedy: A Response to September 11," *Theatre Journal* 54, no. 1 (March 2002): 122.

3. Toni Morrison, *Playing in the Dark: Whiteness and the Literary Imagination* (New York: Vintage, 1993), 46.

4. Jess Row, *White Flights: Race, Fiction, and the American Imagination* (Minneapolis: Graywolf, 2019), 9.

5. Row, *White Flights*, 9.

6. Coco Fusco and José Esteban Muñoz, "A Room of One's Own: Women and Power in the New America," *TDR* 52, no. 1 (Spring 2008): 136–59, https://doi.org/10.1162/dram.2008.52.1.136.

7. Fusco and Muñoz, "A Room of One's Own," 123.

8. Lauren Berlant, *The Anatomy of National Fantasy: Hawthorne, Utopia, and Everyday Life* (Chicago: Chicago University Press, 1991), 1.

9. Richard Blanco, "One Pulse—One Poem," in *Bullets into Bells: Poets and Citizens Respond to Gun Violence*, ed. Brian Clements, Alexandra Teague, and Dean Rader (Boston: Beacon Press, 2017), 18.

10. Roy G. Guzmán, *Catrachos* (Minneapolis: Graywolf, 2019), 49.

11. Pedro Pietri, *Pedro Pietri: Selected Poetry* (San Francisco: City Lights Books, 2015), 3–4.

12. Paul Marcus interviewed by Sylvère Lotringer, *David Wojnarowicz: A Definitive History of Five or Six Years on the Lower East Side*, ed. Giancarlo Ambrosino (Los Angeles: Semiotext(e), 2006), 121.

13. Erica Dawn Lyle, "David Wojnarowicz," *Artforum*, 2018, https://www.artforum.com/events/david-wojnarowicz-4-240860/.

14. Christopher Soto, *Diaries of a Terrorist* (Port Townsend, WA: Copper Canyon Press, 2022), 38.

15. "Mass Shooting Factsheet," Rockefeller Institute of Government, https://rockinst.org/gun-violence/mass-shooting-factsheet/, accessed August 1, 2024.

16. "Explainer," Gun Violence Archive, last edited February 15, 2024, https://www.gunviolencearchive.org/explainer.

17. Marcela Guerrero, *no existe un mundo poshuracán: Puerto Rican Art in the Wake of Hurricane* Maria (New York: Whitney Museum of American Art, 2022), 12.

18. Cherríe Moraga and Gloria Anzaldúa, "Entering the Lives of Others: Theory in the Flesh," in *This Bridge Called My Back: Writings by Radical Women of Color*, ed. Cherríe Moraga and Gloria Anzaldúa (Albany: State University of New York Press, 2015), 19.

19. Maya Chinchilla, "Church at Night," in *Pulse/Pulso: In Remembrance of Orlando*, ed. Roy G. Guzmán and Miguel M. Morales (Richmond, VA: Damaged Goods Press, 2018), 11.

20. Chinchilla, "Church at Night," 9.

21. Eve Kosofsky Sedgwick, *The Weather in Proust*, ed. Jonathan Goldberg (Durham, NC: Duke University Press, 2011), 59.

22. José Esteban Muñoz and Celeste Fraser Delgado, "Rebellions of Everynight Life," in *Everynight Life: Culture and Dance in Latin/o America*, ed. Celeste Fraser Delgado and José Esteban Muñoz (Durham, NC: Duke University Press, 1997), 10.

23. Justin Torres, "In Praise of Latin Night at the Queer Club," *Washington Post*, June 13, 2016.

24. José Esteban Muñoz, "'Gimme Gimme This . . . Gimme Gimme That': *Annihilation and Innovation in the Punk Rock Commons*," *Social Text* 31, no. 3 (Fall 2013): 95–110, https://doi.org/10.1215/01642472-2152855.

25. Muñoz, "A Forum on Theatre and Tragedy," 122.

26. Muñoz, "Gimme Gimme This . . . Gimme Gimme That," 107.

VI: SAINT MUÑOZ

1. José Esteban Muñoz, *The Sense of Brown* (Durham, NC: Duke University Press, 2020), 11.

2. Muñoz, *The Sense of Brown*, 3

3. Roland Barthes, *Roland Barthes by Roland Barthes*, trans. Richard Howard (New York: Hill and Wang, 2010), 94.

4. Jean-Luc Nancy, *Being Singular Plural*, trans. Robert D. Richardson and Anne E. O'Byrne (Stanford: Stanford University Press, 2000), 37.

5. Nancy, *Being Singular Plural*, 61.

6. Muñoz, *The Sense of Brown*, 39.

7. Muñoz, *The Sense of Brown*, 40.

8. Muñoz, *The Sense of Brown*, 149.

9. Muñoz, *The Sense of Brown*, 100.

10. Muñoz, *The Sense of Brown*, 138.

11. Lorgia García-Peña, "Dismantling Anti-Blackness Together," NACLA, June 8, 2020, https://nacla.org/news/2020/06/09/dismantling-anti-blackness-together.

12. José Esteban Muñoz, "The Queer *Social Text*," *Social Text* 27, no. 3 (Fall 2009): 215–18.

13. Lauren Berlant, *The Female Complaint: The Unfinished Business of Sentimentality in American Culture* (Durham, NC Duke University Press, 2008), 9.

14. Muñoz, *The Sense of Brown*, 39.

15. Joshua Javier Guzmán, "Brown," in *Keywords for Latina/o Studies*, ed. Deborah R. Vargas, Nancy Raquel Mirabal, and Lawrence La Fountain-Stokes (New York: New York University Press, 2017), 25.

16. José Esteban Muñoz, "Reviewed Work(s): Negotiating Performance: Gender, Sexuality, and Theatricality in Latin/o America by Diana Taylor and Juan Villegas: El Teatro Campesino: Theatre in the Chicano Movement by Yolanda Broyles-González: Theatre in Latin America: Religion, Politics, and Culture from Cortés to the 1980s by Adam Versényi," *TDR* 41, no. 1 (Spring 1997): 155–58.

17. José Esteban Muñoz, "Toward a Methexic Queer Media," *GLQ* 19, no. 4 (2013): 564.

18. Muñoz, *The Sense of Brown*, 130.

19. Muñoz, *The Sense of Brown*, 121.

20. Muñoz, *The Sense of Brown*, 132.

21. Joshua Chambers-Letson and Tavia Nyong'o, "Introduction," Muñoz, *The Sense of Brown*, xi.

22. Muñoz, *The Sense of Brown*, 123.

23. Jean-Luc Nancy, "The Image: Mimesis and Methexis," in *Nancy and Visual Culture*, ed. Carrie Giunta and Adrienne Janus (Edinburgh: Edinburgh University Press, 2016), 76.

24. Nancy, "The Image," 82–83.

25. Barthes, *Roland Barthes by Roland Barthes*, 3.

26. Hans-Georg Gadamer, *The Gadamer Reader: A Bouquet of the Later Writings*, trans. Richard E. Palmer (Evanston, IL: Northwestern University Press, 2007), 317–19.

27. Gadamer, *The Gadamer Reader*, 313.

28. Muñoz, "Toward a Methexic Queer Media," 564.

29. Muñoz, "Toward a Methexic Queer Media," 564.

30. Muñoz, *The Sense of Brown*, 130.

31. Muñoz, *The Sense of Brown*, 132.

32. Muñoz, *The Sense of Brown*, 127.

33. Lisa Duggan and José Esteban Muñoz, "Hope and Hopelessness: A Dialogue," *Women & Performance: a journal of feminist theory* 19, no. 2 (July 2009): 275–83.

34. Duggan and Muñoz, "Hope and Hopelessness," 273.

35. José Esteban Muñoz, *Cruising Utopia: The Then and There of Queer Futurity, 10th-Anniversary Edition* (New York: New York University Press, 2019), 207.

36. Duggan and Muñoz, "Hope and Hopelessness," 279.

37. Muñoz, *Cruising Utopia, 10th-Anniversary Edition*, 213.

38. José Esteban Muñoz, "Introduction: From Surface to Depth, Between Psychoanalysis and Affect," *Women & Performance: a journal of feminist theory* 19, no. 2 (July 2009): 123–29.

39. José Esteban Muñoz, "Feeling Brown, Feeling Down: Latina Affect, the Performativity of Race, and the Depressive Position," *Signs: Journal of Women and Culture in Society* 31, no. 3 (2006): 675–88.

40. Fred Moten, "the gramsci monument," *Social Text* 32, no. 1 (Spring 2014): 117–18.

41. Moten, "the gramsci monument," 117.

42. José Esteban Muñoz, "The Event of the Poem: 'the gramsci monument,'" *Social Text* 32, no. 1 (Spring 2014): 121.

43. K'eguro Macharia, *Frottage: Frictions of Intimacy Across the Black Diaspora* (New York: New York University Press, 2019), 166.

44. Lauren Berlant, *Desire/Love* (Brooklyn, NY: Punctum Books, 2012), 112.

45. Eve Kosofsky Sedgwick, *Bathroom Songs: Eve Kosofsky Sedgwick as a Poet*, ed. Jason Edwards (Brooklyn, NY: Punctum Books, 2017), 208.

Index